AMERICA the BEAUTIFUL

FLORIDA

By Lynn M. Stone

Consultants

Randall G. Felton, Ph.D., High School Curriculum Program Specialist, Leon County Schools, Tallahassee

Peter D. Klingman, Ph.D., Dean, Resource Development/International Education, Daytona Beach Community College, Daytona Beach

David A. Bice, M.A., Author of *A Panorama of Florida*

Robert L. Hillerich, Ph.D., Bowling Green State University, Bowling Green, Ohio

CHILDRENS PRESS ®

CHICAGO

Alligators can be found in some of Florida's ponds, lakes, rivers, and swamps (above).

Project Editor: Joan Downing
Assistant Editor: Shari Joffe
Design Director: Margrit Fiddle
Typesetting: Graphic Connections, Inc.
Engraving: Liberty Photoengraving

Library of Congress Cataloging-in-Publication Data

Stone, Lynn M.
   America the beautiful. Florida.

   (America the beautiful state books)
   Includes index.
   Summary: Introduces the geography, history,
government, economy, industry, culture, historic sites,
and famous people of the Sunshine State.
   1. Florida—Juvenile literature. [1. Florida]
I. Title. II. Series.
F311.3.S76 1987   975.9   87-9391
ISBN 0-516-00455-7

Biscayne Boulevard in downtown Miami

TABLE OF CONTENTS

Chapter 1

THE SUNSHINE STATE

THE SUNSHINE STATE

Florida. The name calls up postcard pictures of blue-green seas lapping against sandy beaches, palms ruffled by tropical breezes, stately gardens, fiery sunsets, and people outdoors—always outdoors. In most states, a town called Frostproof would be a joke. But Florida is a state quite unlike any other, and it is, perhaps more than any other, everyone's state. If spending time in the Sunshine State is not *the* American dream, it is surely one of them. Florida's year-round warm weather, high percentage of sunny days, beaches, theme parks, and natural beauty beckon millions of visitors every year.

Despite the growing skylines of its cities and its image as a resort—hallmarks of twentieth-century progress—Florida has not always been the tourist's haven it is today. Its roots lie deep in a stormy history flavored by bitter and bloody international rivalries, pirates, slavery, Indian wars, segregation, the Civil War, and environmental mismanagement. Relics of Florida's past can be both fascinating and grim.

Too often, Florida is portrayed as a giant, sun-drenched sandbox or an enormous park. There is sand, to be sure, as well as the largest concentration of parks on the planet. But the real substance of Florida is what even the most colorful postcards rarely capture: the immense variety of its wildlife, economic endeavors, landscape, and people—and their culture, tradition, and history.

Chapter 2

THE LAND

THE LAND

Those who never leave Florida, and those who leave but always come back, are said to have "sand in their shoes." That thought speaks not only of people with an incurable affection for Florida, it also says something of the character of the land. Sandy beaches and sandy soils are a feature of much of Florida. Yet to dismiss the Florida landscape as a long sand trap would be a mistake. Florida's landscape is uncommonly lush, punctuated by deep forests, springs, rivers, lakes, and vast wetlands.

GEOGRAPHY AND TOPOGRAPHY

Geologists think that Florida may be the youngest part of the United States. Florida emerged from the sea, more or less in its present form, only ten thousand years ago.

The state of Florida is the highest part of the Florida Plateau, a platform extending like a partially submerged pier from the North American continent. Florida rises gently from the sea, rarely exceeding more than 325 feet (99 meters) above sea level at any point. The plateau itself is one of the most stable sections of the earth's crust, but the rise and fall of the seas have alternately submerged and exposed parts of it for millions of years.

Florida is not a large state. Covering 54,090 square miles (140,098 square kilometers), it ranks twenty-sixth among the states in size. But it contains great distances because of its long

Much of the Florida landscape, including this area along the Myakka River near the Gulf coast, is uncommonly lush.

peninsula and panhandle. Its greatest distance from north to south is 447 miles (719 kilometers); its greatest distance from east to west is 361 miles (581 kilometers).

The state's topography varies very little. In general, north and central Florida are rolling, and south Florida is flat. The highest point in the state, in northern Walton County near the Alabama border, is only 345 feet (105 meters) above sea level.

NATURAL REGIONS

Florida is often divided into six natural regions. The Coastal Lowlands include the entire coast and the Florida Keys. The Lowlands are uniformly flat, but as they extend inland from the shore, they include a variety of natural habitats: forest, prairie, swamp, and sand dune. Reaching inland as far as sixty miles (ninety-seven kilometers), the Coastal Lowlands are home to almost all of Florida's major commercial, industrial, and resort centers.

The Western Highlands in the northwestern Florida panhandle are relatively hilly. They are notched by several narrow, steep-walled valleys. The land there is sparsely settled, and much of it is covered by thick pine forests.

The Marianna Lowlands are in the north-central part of the panhandle, west of the Apalachicola River in Washington, Holmes, and Jackson counties. This is hilly country, too, but the hills are low and rolling, and the region is pocked by a large number of sinkholes. Cotton is produced in this area.

Rolling hills and gentle slopes are typical of the Tallahassee Hills region. It occupies part of the eastern panhandle and extends north of Tallahassee to the Georgia border.

The Central Highlands occupy much of the central Florida peninsula from the Georgia state line and Okefenokee Swamp south to a point just north of Lake Okeechobee. Much of this region, particularly the area south of Ocala, consists of rolling hills and thousands of lakes.

Two separate swamplands make up the sixth type of geographical region in Florida. The Big Cypress and the Everglades together virtually cover the southern tip of Florida. Okefenokee is a huge swamp that straddles the Georgia-Florida border. Although it stretches over 660 square miles (1,709 square kilometers), only 66 square miles (171 square kilometers) of it extend into Florida.

THE COASTS

A straight line drawn down Florida's saltwater coasts would be 580 miles (933 kilometers) long on the Atlantic Ocean side and 770 miles (1,239 kilometers) long on the Gulf of Mexico side. Charting the indentations, however, the total is 8,426 miles

Swampland (bottom right) and clumps of mangroves
(top right) are features of the Everglades (left),
a vast wetland that spreads over the southern tip
of Florida.

(13,557 kilometers). Only Alaska, among the states, has a longer
shore. No place in Florida is more than 60 miles (97 kilometers)
from salt water.

The sand beaches so popular with "snowbirds," the tourists
who flee northern winters, account for less than half of Florida's
coast. Most of the coast consists of swamps, marshes, and muddy
bays. A few beaches, such as the Point of Rocks on Siesta Key,
near Sarasota, have natural rock outcrops, but rocky beaches are
unusual in Florida. Not so unusual are the mangrove swamps on
Florida's southern coasts. A mangrove is a type of tree that is able
to thrive in water and soil with a high salt content. When exposed
by low tides, their fingerlike roots look like grotesquely jointed
stilts.

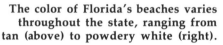

The color of Florida's beaches varies throughout the state, ranging from tan (above) to powdery white (right).

Florida's central and northern coasts have huge salt marshes. These low, wet lands look like hay fields. The "hay" is actually juncus and spartina grass, which can survive daily flooding by saltwater tides. Just beyond the marshes, in saltwater bays, are submerged gardens of turtle grass.

Florida's sandy shores may be dazzling white, a shade of tan, or even gray. The state's powdery white beaches, such as those near Panama City, are nearly 100 percent quartz sand. The gray tone of Venice beach is due to large amounts of organic compounds called phosphates. Tan beaches, common on the east coast, reflect high shell and iron content.

Whatever their color, Florida's beaches have become increasingly crowded in recent years. Keeping them "healthy" is a growing problem. When the plant life of the upper beach is destroyed, the sands shift and blow. Sea walls, erected to protect beach property, have created problems for marine life. Lawmakers

Florida's largest river, the St. Johns, is one of the few rivers in the United States that flows from south to north.

are becoming careful about regulating construction so the beaches can be preserved in their natural condition.

THE WETLANDS

Approximately 4,470 square miles (11,577 kilometers) of the Florida land mass is covered by fresh water. The State Division of Water Resources lists 7,712 lakes of 10 acres (4 hectares) or more. The total tops 30,000 when smaller bodies of water are counted. The biggest is Lake Okeechobee, the third-largest freshwater lake wholly within the United States and the second-largest freshwater lake entirely within the boundaries of one state. It covers about 700 square miles (1,800 square kilometers). Like several other large Florida lakes—Apopka, Istokpoga, Crescent, George, and Monroe among them—Lake Okeechobee fills a shallow depression that was once a sea bottom. Its average depth is only 6 to 10 feet (1.8 to 3 meters).

The largest of Florida's thirty-four major rivers is the St. Johns. From its start near Melbourne, the St. Johns flows 273 miles

(439 kilometers) north to Jacksonville. Northwestern Florida's most important river is the Apalachicola. The most famous river in Florida is the Suwannee. Although he never saw the river himself, Stephen Foster guaranteed the dark, slow-moving Suwannee a spot in American hearts with the lyrics to "Old Folks at Home," the tune that became Florida's state song.

Many places have sinkholes, but Florida has more than its share. Sinkholes develop when underground water acts over a long period of time on a limestone surface above, eventually causing the limestone to erode and collapse. The hole that results, a water-filled pit that "wasn't there yesterday," is a sinkhole. Devil's Millhopper, a well-known sinkhole in Gainesville, is 118 feet (36 meters) deep and 500 feet (152 meters) wide.

At least forty-six of Florida's sixty-seven counties contain springs. Wakulla Springs near Tallahassee is 185 feet (56 meters) deep, making it one of the deepest springs in the country. Silver Springs, the largest spring in the state, is one of central Florida's main tourist attractions.

Florida's most distinctive wetlands are the Everglades. A wilderness of limestone rock, muck, sawgrass, hammocks (tree islands), and gently flowing water, the Everglades are what author Marjory Stoneman Douglas called a "river of grass." The Everglades are about 100 miles (161 kilometers) long and 30 miles (48 kilometers) wide. They cover 2,746 square miles (7,112 square kilometers) south of Lake Okeechobee and west of Miami.

Part of the Everglades has been drained so that the rich soil underneath can be used for farms. Keeping farm interests happy while maintaining enough water in the Everglades for wildlife has been a problem of growing concern. In the early 1980s, Governor Bob Graham began a costly program to help restore water to the Everglades.

Wetlands in Florida include crystal-clear springs such as Silver Springs in central Florida (left), and sinkholes such as this one in Winter Park (above).

SUNSHINE AND RAIN

On the average, two-thirds of Florida's days are sunny. In the 1920s, the *St. Petersburg Independent* began giving away newspapers on any day when the sun did not shine at all—and the *Independent* had no intention of losing money.

Florida summers are long, humid, and warm. The state's highest recorded temperature was 109 degrees Fahrenheit (43 degrees Celsius) at Monticello on June 29, 1931. Temperatures over 100 degrees Fahrenheit (37 degrees Celsius) are rare. The humidity, however, makes Florida summers seem hotter than they actually are. July temperatures in both Tallahassee and Miami average 82 degrees Fahrenheit (28 degrees Celsius). Winters are mild, though often interrupted by cool or cold air from the north. The average January temperature is 54 degrees Fahrenheit (12 degrees Celsius) in northern Florida and 67 degrees Fahrenheit (19 degrees Celsius) in southern Florida.

Florida's warm weather is one of its greatest natural assets. Yet no place on the mainland is entirely safe from the possibility of

Summer rains account for about 50 percent of Florida's yearly rainfall.

frost and freezing temperatures. Cold waves, however, seldom last more than a day or two, and rarely penetrate into southern Florida. A record low of minus 2 degrees Fahrenheit (minus 17 degrees Celsius) was reached at Tallahassee on February 13, 1899.

Rainfall averages from 50 inches (128 centimeters) to 65 inches (166 centimeters) per year, depending on location. The highest rainfall occurs in the extreme northwest corner of the state and at the southern tip of the peninsula. The Florida Keys, south of the peninsula, receive an annual rainfall of 40 inches (102 centimeters).

While Floridians do not worry about blizzards, violent windstorms and rainstorms are another matter. No state has more thunderstorms, and Fort Myers averages one hundred days with lightning per year. Florida is also one of the ten most-tornado-prone states. Between June and October, Florida is subject to hurricanes. They usually form in the Caribbean Sea or Atlantic Ocean, traveling north along the Gulf and Atlantic coasts. Low-lying coastal areas can be battered badly by winds, high waves, and floods.

Left: A bald cypress forest in Corkscrew Swamp
Above: Yellow coreopsis in bloom on a Florida prairie

FOREST, SCRUB, AND PRAIRIE

Despite its consistently low elevation, the Florida landscape boasts an amazing variety of plant life—approximately thirty-five hundred species. Only Texas and California have more. Nearly half of all the species of trees found in the United States grow in Florida. And even though timber was among Florida's earliest industries, about 50 percent of the state remains forested. Coniferous pines, so important in Florida's lumber production, dominate some woodlands. Hardwood trees such as oaks, bays, swamp maples, and bald cypresses dominate others. Still other forests are a blend of several species and types. Many woodlands are laced with sabal palms, the state tree. Sabal palms are also known as cabbage palms because the bud of the tree was commonly used as a vegetable in the early days of Florida settlement. Even today, "swamp cabbage" is prepared by some Floridians.

In the lower Florida peninsula and in the Keys are dozens of species of subtropical trees. The exceptionally warm climate here is ideal for such species as strangler fig, paurotis palm, royal palm, and mangroves. The gumbo limbo of southern Florida is called the "tourist tree" because its bark peels like sunburned skin.

19

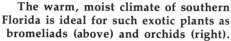
The warm, moist climate of southern Florida is ideal for such exotic plants as bromeliads (above) and orchids (right).

Another unique Florida forest is the "scrub" of central Florida. The dry scrub forest developed on sand dunes left exposed thousands of years ago when the sea level dropped. Florida scrub country is relatively high and its sandy soil drains easily, so much of it has been developed and converted into citrus groves.

Undeveloped Florida is not all woodland or wetland. The state also has prairies—broad expanses of wild grasses and flowers with few trees. Like the famous midwestern prairies, Florida's grasslands are the home of burrowing owls, sandhill cranes, and even cowboys.

Wildflowers grow throughout Florida's undeveloped lands. Among the most unusual are the bromeliads, air plants that grow on trees and take nourishment from the air and rain without injuring the host tree. Bromeliads and other plants grow in overwhelming numbers in the bald cypress forests of southern Florida. The familiar Spanish moss of Florida and the South is not really moss but a type of air plant. Florida also has large numbers of wild orchids. Most of them grow only in the southern part of the state.

The more than four hundred species of birds that can be found in Florida include the sandhill crane (above) and the brown pelican (right).

FLORIDA: FOR THE BIRDS

More than one hundred native species of birds have been recorded in Florida, and nearly three hundred species nest in the state or regularly pass through during migration.

The most popular of Florida's birds is the brown pelican. Brown pelicans are regular fixtures on the jetties, piers, and bridges of the coasts. Though they can make spectacular offshore dives for their dinner, they waddle about the docks, unafraid, and wait for handouts of fish. The state's wetlands are also the haunts of wood storks; wading birds such as herons and egrets; wood ducks; and roseate spoonbills, the long-legged pink birds often mistaken for flamingos. Ospreys, white pelicans, and southern bald eagles fish lakes, rivers, and bays. Terns, cormorants, and black skimmers

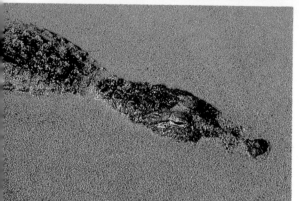

Among the many species of land and sea animals that live in Florida are (clockwise from top left) the roseate spoonbill, the purple gallinule, the ghost crab, the Florida panther, the Key deer, the coral snake, the manatee, the green sea turtle, and the American alligator.

fish offshore. Oystercatchers, sanderlings, and plovers busily work the beaches. Florida's woodlands are home to wild turkeys, quail, woodpeckers, and owls. The mockingbird, Florida's state bird, can be found in suburban areas.

MAMMALS

Some ninety mammal species live in Florida. Many are those found also in the North—bobcat, opossum, striped skunk, gray fox, otter, beaver, whitetail deer, gray squirrel, black bear, and raccoon, to name a few. Other species of animals are found only in Florida. Two of the rarest and best known of these are the Key deer and Florida panther.

Key deer are found only in the lower Florida Keys. They look like junior editions of the larger whitetails found on the Florida peninsula. The Florida panther, the state animal, has a sanctuary in the Big Cypress Swamp and in Everglades National Park, but even these immense wildernesses may not be enough to save it. This large cat, a southern variety of the mountain lion, is extremely rare. Some panthers have been killed accidentally while crossing Interstate 75 in the Big Cypress. Underground crossings have been constructed for the panthers in hopes that the remaining few—perhaps twenty—will avoid the road.

One of the most unusual animals in Florida is the West Indian manatee, or "sea cow." The manatee is not actually a cow, but an aquatic mammal that has flippers instead of legs. Manatees are docile creatures that live on a strictly vegetarian diet. They are found in saltwater bays, and in the winter, in freshwater lagoons and springs. A more familiar sight in Florida coastal waters is the bottle-nosed porpoise. Frolicking and rolling in the waves, porpoises delight beachcombers and boaters.

REPTILES AND AMPHIBIANS

Endangered by illegal hunting in the 1960s and 1970s, alligators have made a stunning comeback. In Florida, alligators live in swamps, ponds, lakes, and rivers. Florida also has American crocodiles. These creatures are extremely rare, and can be found only in the coastal edges of Everglades National Park and the Upper Florida Keys, especially Key Largo.

Gopher tortoises and box turtles live in the uplands. Sea turtles come ashore each spring and summer to nest on dark beaches. Several species of sea turtle nest in Florida, but the loggerhead, which can weigh more than 300 pounds (136 kilograms) is by far the most common. Though most snakes in Florida are harmless to people, poisonous species include rattlesnakes, coral snakes, cottonmouths, and copperheads. A "new" frog, previously unknown to science, was discovered in the hill-and-gully country of the Florida panhandle in 1982. State biologist Paul Moler, who knew all the songs of Florida's frogs and toads, heard a call he did not recognize. He found the mystery singer, and it turned out to be a previously unrecognized species. It is now known as the Florida bog frog.

FISH AND INVERTEBRATES

The king of Florida's freshwater fish, at least to anglers, is the largemouth bass. Various relatives of the black bass, collectively known as sunfish and including crappies, bream, and bluegills, also live in fresh water.

In the bays and saltwater creeks, snook, tarpon, redfish, and sea trout are among the bigger fish. Grouper, Atlantic sailfish, jewfish, dolphin, red snapper, and kingfish are important deep-sea fish.

The Portuguese man-of-war (left), a balloonlike sea creature whose tentacles cause a painful sting, can often be found washed up on Florida beaches. The Florida bog frog (above) is a recently discovered species.

Florida's coastal waters are also home to hundreds of kinds of marine invertebrates. These saltwater invertebrates come in many shapes, sizes, and colors. Many of them are easily seen in shallow bays during low tide. They include urchins, starfish, sand dollars, sea horses, crabs, Florida lobsters, and a variety of sea snails. The biggest of these is the Florida horse conch, which is Florida's state shell and one of the largest marine mollusks in the world.

Floridians have learned to avoid the many species of jellyfish that live in Florida's waters. Their tentacles can inflict painful welts on unsuspecting arms and legs. The Portuguese man-of-war is a beautiful creature that floats in the ocean like a translucent balloon. But beware this animal's long, trailing tentacles.

FLORIDA ANIMALS IN THE TWENTIETH CENTURY

Several of Florida's animals are on lists of endangered animals put out by the state and federal governments. These include the American crocodile, wood stork, manatee, southern bald eagle, Florida panther, mangrove fox squirrel, dusky seaside sparrow, and red-cockaded woodpecker.

The state of Florida has set aside thousands of acres of land to protect wildlife and has begun to purchase "critical" lands, those of considerable ecological value. Between 1978 and 1986, Florida spent about $700 million on land purchases.

Chapter 3
THE PEOPLE

THE PEOPLE

It has been said that Florida is the only northern state in the Deep South. Actually, an old Florida adage is probably more accurate: if you draw a line across the state's center from Allandale to Yankeetown, everything south of it is northern and everything north of it is southern.

Though it is, of course, a sweeping generalization, there is some truth to that idea. As Florida's population has shifted southward, it has been swelled by transplants from the North. Many of the resort cities in south Florida were developed in the twentieth century by northerners. The interior towns, however, particularly those in north Florida, were settled early and have escaped some of the rapid development and population explosions experienced in south Florida. Whereas much of north Florida retains the aura of the Old South, the population centers of south Florida tend to reflect more-northern attitudes.

POPULATION

In the early nineteenth century, the southern half of the Florida peninsula was wilderness country. Virtually uninhabited, it was dominated by the Everglades and low-lying jungle forests known as hammocks. But already people of vision were looking toward south Florida—and the future. In 1847, the government dispatched Buckingham Smith of St. Augustine to the Everglades

People over the age of sixty-five make up nearly 20 percent of Florida's population.

region to determine if the area could be "reclaimed and made valuable." Smith estimated that no more than fifty white persons were living south of Lake Okeechobee, and reported that "a population of perhaps 250,000 can ultimately live in the reclaimed region." Today, the "Everglades counties" of the southeast coast — Dade, Broward, and Palm Beach — have over 3.5 million people. That is over one-third of Florida's total population, which was 9,746,621 when the 1980 census was taken.

Those counties have not been alone in their growth. The state as a whole grew faster between 1970 and 1980 than all other states except Arizona and Nevada. Most Florida growth has been on its central and lower coasts. Eight of the state's ten largest cities lie there, though the state's largest city, Jacksonville, is on the North Atlantic coast.

As the coasts have developed, bolstered by tourism and the lure of seaside living, Florida's population has become more urban. Eighty-four percent of the population is classified as urban. The greatest density is in the sprawling, southeast urban complex between Miami and West Palm Beach. Orlando, the Cape Canaveral area, and Daytona Beach form another large metropolitan area in east-central Florida. Tampa, Clearwater, and St. Petersburg represent a large, dense population center on the west coast. Still, compared to other states, Florida's density is only moderate, averaging about 192 people per square mile (74 per square kilometer). However, the population density varies throughout the state. Whereas coastal cities are heavily populated, the state's interior remains relatively open. Much of central Florida, with the exception of the Orlando area, is vast stretches of pasture, swamp, and forest lying between small towns.

CRACKERS AND YANKEES

As Florida has grown, it has attracted immigrants from many states and countries. The earliest European settlers were sixteenth-century Spaniards. The first large numbers of white settlers who stayed, however, were English colonists from Georgia and the Carolinas. When Florida was taken over from Spain by the United States in 1822, American settlers began to arrive from Alabama and Georgia. Now most of the state's "new" population is from the Northeast and the Midwest. Florida has also attracted a large number of refugees and immigrants from Caribbean nations. The combination creates a truly cosmopolitan population.

Most of Florida's population is white and American-born. Its two largest groups, nicknamed Yankees and Crackers, comprise 50 to 70 percent of the population. To native Floridians, Yankees are immigrants from the Midwest and Northeast. Crackers, by a broad definition, are those born in Georgia or Florida, or by a narrow definition, the descendants of Florida's early farmers and plantation owners. Some say the name comes from the loud crack of bull whips when the farmers drove their cattle. Some Floridians dislike the name, because it has sometimes been used as a disparaging term for poor, southern whites.

By anyone's definition, Ken Alvarez is a Cracker. He was born and grew up in central Florida. He has munched on hearts of palm, milked rattlesnakes, dined on barbecued wild pig, and formed low opinions of Miami Beach, high-rise apartments, and the Bahia grass that dominates the tidy yards of subdivisions. He is the descendant of an immigrant who left Spain in 1771 and settled in Florida in the early 1800s.

Alvarez knows he is one of a vanishing breed. He has seen his home state—and town—change dramatically. "I grew up in the Old South," he says, "but that's pretty much gone in Florida. You have to go up into northern Florida, into the interior parts of the panhandle, to find that now." The Florida of the 1940s, which Alvarez knew as a child, was not very cosmopolitan by 1980 standards. "Florida was until recently basically a state of small towns," he says, "really a rural state, a cowboy state. Cattle didn't have to be kept behind fences here until 1950. It was a different mentality and a different world."

For Florida Crackers, the influx of Yankees has been a mixed blessing. Alvarez, a regional interpretive naturalist for the state's Department of Natural Resources, is particularly sensitive about environmental changes. "Water," he says, as a case in point, "is something we need more of. We use more of it, but there's less and less of it, and it costs more all the time." With a twinkle in his eye, he likens the Yankee invasion to bad weather. "It just comes," he said, "but you learn to adjust to it."

Alvarez is quick to point out that the "new" Florida is not without virtue. "We live in a wealthier state now, one with far more opportunities." He and thousands of other native Floridians are proud of their state's new sophistication. Throughout all the changes, Florida's great weather has stayed the same, and people like Alvarez have no intention of leaving just because the cattle are behind fences nowadays.

Cuban men playing dominoes in the park (left) are a common sight in Little Havana (above), the center of Miami's large Cuban community.

ETHNIC FLORIDA

Among ethnic minorities in Florida, the largest is the black population. About 14 percent of the resident population is black. The history of black people in Florida dates at least as far back as that of whites. Blacks were among the first Spanish explorers to visit the state in the sixteenth century. Later, largely in the eighteenth century, a few runaway slaves from Georgia and the Carolinas accompanied the immigration of Seminole Indians into Florida. When Florida became United States property, the number of blacks quickly increased because American settlers brought them as slaves.

While the number of black Floridians increased dramatically under the United States flag, the number of Seminole Indians decreased just as dramatically. About 5,000 Seminole lived in Florida at the time of United States annexation. Within twenty-five years, following a governmental policy of forced removal, the

In the late 1970s and early 1980s, thousands of Haitian refugees flooded into Florida to escape poverty and dictatorship at home.

Seminole population had shrunk to about 150. Today there are some 1,500 Seminole in Florida, the majority of whom live on reservations in Immokalee, Hollywood, Brighton, near the Big Cypress Swamp, and in Hillsborough County.

About 9 percent of Florida's population is Hispanic, mostly of Cuban origin. Cubans began arriving in Florida in large numbers in 1868. Spurred by revolutionary warfare in Cuba, Vincente Martinez Ybor moved his cigar factories—and workers—from Havana to Key West. In 1886, after a fire and labor unrest in Key West, Ybor moved his operation and employees to Tampa.

Fidel Castro's revolution in Cuba in the late 1950s triggered a flood of 350,000 Cuban refugees. About one-third of the refugees settled in Florida, largely in the Miami area, during the 1960s. When Castro let Cubans leave again in 1980, about 80,000 more settled in Miami's Hispanic community. In 1981, hundreds of Haitians fleeing the Duvalier regime landed in small boats at and near Key West. In a controversial action by the United States government, many of them were detained as illegal aliens at various compounds and not released until a year later.

Settlers from northern Spain were attracted to Tampa in the early 1900s by the cigar industry and by previously established Spanish-speaking neighborhoods. Tarpon Springs became a center for Greek immigrants who worked in the sponge industry. Florida also has large communities from Italy, the United Kingdom, Germany, the Soviet Union, and Czechoslovakia.

The largest single religious affiliation of Floridians is Roman Catholic, although Protestants of many different denominations outnumber Catholics. Baptists and Methodists are the largest Protestant groups. Florida also has a sizable Jewish community centered in the Miami area.

TRENDS IN THE EIGHTIES

During the 1970s, while the nation grew 11.4 percent as a whole, Florida's population grew 43.5 percent. People over sixty-five, most of them retired, make up nearly 20 percent of the resident population, well over the national average of 11 percent. Florida's median age of 34.7 years, according to the 1980 census, makes it the "oldest" state in the nation.

The obvious lure of Florida for retirees is the weather. Affordability is another factor. While real-estate prices rocketed up in many regions of the country during the past few years, Florida's building costs remained quite stable.

Florida has catered to its retired population for years. It has a legion of retirement villages that offer golf, tennis, swimming, public transportation, shuffleboard, games, and—perhaps best of all—camaraderie. These communities help smooth the way for thousands of incoming senior citizens each year. Between 1970 and 1980, Florida's over-sixty-five population nearly doubled the state's overall growth rate.

Chapter 4

THE BEGINNING

THE BEGINNING

Originally from Ohio, Bob Pelham has lived in Sarasota since 1951. In Florida, where newcomers are commonplace, he is an old-timer. But on his bookcase resides a real old-timer—a human skull that is about five thousand years old. The skull was plucked from the muddy sands of Little Salt Spring. Since 1959, scientists have been diving into the warm, clear waters of the spring and discovering the remains and artifacts of ancient Floridians.

THE FIRST FLORIDIANS

No one knows exactly when people first lived in Florida. The remains from Little Salt Spring, as old as they are, are probably not the bones of Florida's first native people. Most scientists think that Indians first might have lived in Florida ten thousand years ago. Some scholars think that the first Floridians were descendants of Asians who pushed southward through North America after crossing from Siberia into Alaska twenty thousand years ago. But archaeological evidence linking early Floridians to Central and South American groups have led other scholars to theorize that Florida's earliest people migrated from the south. The oldest semipermanent villages that have been unearthed are approximately five thousand years old.

The first people in Florida were hunters. They used wooden spears with stone points to kill many kinds of large mammals that

Timucuan Indians as portrayed by a French artist who visited Florida in 1564

are now extinct. Later, around 5000 B.C., the people became more dependent on shellfish and began to create simple villages. Florida Indians were making pottery by 2000 B.C., eight hundred years before any other American people. A thousand years later they began producing some of their own food, depending less on hunting and gathering.

By about two thousand years ago, Florida Indians were apparently traveling and trading extensively. Burial mounds in Florida have revealed artifacts that look the same as those used by ancient people of Ohio and Illinois. The northern mounds, in turn, have revealed conch shells, presumably from Florida.

When the Spaniards began landing in Florida in the early sixteenth century, Florida had between ten thousand and twenty-five thousand Indians. The major groups were known as the Calusa, Apalachee, Timucua, and Tequesta. Juan Ponce de León, a Spanish noble, adventurer, and explorer, is credited as the first European to discover Florida. In just two-and-a-half centuries after his first visit in 1513, almost all of Florida's native people were gone. Some died from diseases brought by Europeans. Others died in battle with the newcomers or were taken away by slave catchers. Some migrated elsewhere.

Fortunately, they did not disappear without a trace. Ancient burial mounds and shell mounds can still be seen in Florida. The University of Miami, which now owns Little Salt Spring, still sends divers down among the turtles and alligators to collect relics from the recesses of the spring.

SPANISH SETTLEMENT

Ponce de León's discovery of Florida in April 1513 came when the powerful European nations, Spain among them, were seeking new trade routes and new lands to conquer. Spain had already made inroads in the New World, and Ponce de León himself had explored and conquered Puerto Rico in 1508. Legend says that Ponce de León was a man driven to exploration by his desire to find the mysterious Fountain of Youth. Actually, the fountain probably played little, if any, role in Ponce de León's ambitions. Like other Spanish explorers, he was motivated primarily by the possibility of finding gold and new land for governing.

Ponce de León's experience in Florida must have been a personal disappointment. He did discover the area, and he named it *Florida*, which in Spanish means "full of flowers." His exploration also turned up the Bahama Channel, the sea-lane later used by the Spanish fleet to sail from the Caribbean Sea to the Atlantic. But there was no gold in Florida, and, if it mattered, no Fountain of Youth. There were plenty of native people, but they did not welcome the newcomers. When Ponce de León made a second journey to Florida in 1521 to begin a colony, he was wounded during a battle against these Indians and was forced to

Spanish exploration of Florida began with Ponce de León (above), who gave the area its name, and continued with Hernando De Soto's difficult expedition through the region in 1539 (left).

abandon settlement plans. A short time later, he died of his injuries, an event that foreshadowed almost three hundred years of often-futile Spanish involvement in Florida.

Another Spaniard, Pánfilo de Narváez, attempted a Florida settlement in 1528. De Narváez failed when many of his ships were wrecked in a storm. In 1539, Hernando De Soto, one of the great Spanish *conquistadores* (conquerors), tried his hand in Florida. De Soto and several hundred well-armed Spaniards sailed into Tampa Bay, landing somewhere near the present-day city of Bradenton. De Soto and his men traveled up the center of Florida looking for the cities of gold they had seen in Peru, but they encountered only wilderness and Indian attacks. Occasionally the men in the Spanish camp awoke to a gruesome sight—one of their number, beheaded, hanging from a nearby tree. Indian harassment was trying, but the swamps and marshes were worse. De Soto's band, exhausted and disheartened, pushed north out of Florida.

While De Soto's men fought through Florida, two Spanish rivals, France and England, were building strength at home and kindling interest in the New World. The wealth Spain had taken

Fort Caroline (left), built by a group of French Huguenots who had come to Florida in 1564, was destroyed when the French were massacred by Spanish settlers who had been sent to reclaim the area for Spain (below). Nearby, the Spanish built St. Augustine (below left), which was to become the first permanent European settlement in what is today the United States.

from Central and South America tempted the French and the English to try their luck in North America. The French reasoned that Florida would be a good place from which to attack Spanish trading ships. In 1564, a group of French Protestants called Huguenots, led by René de Goulaine de Laudonnière, established Fort Caroline and a colony near present-day Jacksonville at the mouth of the St. Johns River. Spain feared that France would gain a toehold in Florida, which Spain considered her property.

King Philip II of Spain sent an able seaman, Don Pedro Menéndez de Avilés, to drive the French out of Florida. Menéndez and four hundred soldiers arrived in Florida in 1565. They attacked Fort Caroline and massacred the French colonists. Near the destroyed French settlement, Menéndez founded St. Augustine, which became the first permanent European settlement in what is today the United States.

France did not attempt another permanent settlement in Florida again until the late 1600s, and then it chose the upper Gulf coast. Today, the only reminder of the Fort Caroline colony is a monument on the St. Johns River near Jacksonville.

TROUBLE WITH ENGLAND

Though France was no longer a threat in Florida, Spain's problems there were far from over. England loomed as the next danger. In 1586, English seafarer Sir Francis Drake burned and looted St. Augustine. Drake's raid was typical of the British hit-and-run raids that would follow. Then England successfully settled Jamestown, Virginia in 1607, Charleston, South Carolina in 1670, and Savannah, Georgia, in 1733.

The government of Spain eyed these growing settlements with considerable worry. But it did not try to stop them. Rather, Spain elected to strengthen its position in Florida. Part of its strategy was to convert Florida's Indians to Christianity, and to convince them to side with Spain against the British. Both efforts met with only moderate success. In 1672, Spain began construction of Castillo de San Marcos, an enormous stone fort that still stands in St. Augustine. The fort gave the Spanish a military base with which to counter the British port at Charleston.

By 1628, Spain had become alarmed once again by French activity in North America. French advances along the upper Gulf coast prompted Spain to hurriedly build a wooden fort at what is today Pensacola. Although the French seized and briefly held

Castillo de San Marcos, a massive fort built by the Spanish between 1672 and 1695, withstood repeated assaults by the British during the early 1700s.

Pensacola in 1719, they were really more interested in the Mississippi River Valley than in Florida.

On the Atlantic coast, the English in Carolina and Georgia felt threatened by the Spanish presence in Florida. The fact that their countries were often officially at war in Europe gave both sides an excuse for warfare in North America. Carolina Governor James Moore directed an attack on St. Augustine in 1702. The residents and defenders of St. Augustine gathered behind the 12-foot- (3.6-meter-) thick walls of the stone fort. Spanish warships from Havana rushed north and blocked Moore's ships in the harbor, forcing him to retreat by land. Moore, however, returned to Florida with Indian allies and destroyed the chain of Spanish missions in north Florida. The frontier was now undefended by Spain.

The fort at St. Augustine survived two more major British assaults. General James Oglethorpe of Georgia attacked in 1740. When seven Spanish warships appeared on the horizon, Oglethorpe gave up the attack. He tried again in 1742, but his attack fleet was scattered by storms and he had to abandon the effort. In between Oglethorpe's raids on St. Augustine, Spain attacked plantations in Georgia and Carolina and sailed thirty captured British ships into St. Augustine harbor in 1741. Spain considered a major attack on Charleston, but never carried it out.

Spain's grasp on Florida was weak. It had neither soldiers, missionaries, nor traders enough to control the Indians, much less the British. Many thousands of Indians had been carried away by slavers. Those who remained preferred French and English goods to Spanish. By 1763, after 250 years of colonization in Florida, Spain had only St. Augustine in the east, a struggling settlement at Pensacola in the west, and a little military force at St. Marks on the upper Gulf coast. In between were Indians, British and French traders, and wilderness.

Although Florida was still of some value as an outpost from which Spain could guard its Caribbean fleets, it was becoming increasingly costly to defend. In 1763, the Seven Years' War in Europe ended. The Treaty of Paris, which tried to sort out the results, gave Florida to England. In exchange for Florida, Spain received Havana, which had been captured by the British.

UNDER THE UNION JACK

England separated the Florida territory into East and West Florida. Pensacola was the capital of the west, which included the region west of the Apalachicola River and parts of what are now Alabama, Mississippi, and Louisiana. East Florida consisted of lands east of the Apalachicola, with St. Augustine as the capital.

The British lured colonists to Florida by offering generous land grants and financial help with exports. But British rule was short-lived. By 1776 England was contending with the American Revolution. Thousands of Loyalists (British sympathizers) fled from Georgia and the Carolinas into East Florida. Most British colonists in East Florida, generally unaffected by the discontent "up north," remained loyal to England. In St. Augustine, Loyalists burned likenesses of American revolutionary heroes John Hancock and Samuel Adams.

The war itself was fought, for the most part, far north of Florida. There were no pitched battles between English and American forces in East Florida, although there were occasional raids. In West Florida, the Spanish took advantage of Britain's preoccupation with the colonies and marched into West Florida in 1779. Pensacola was captured in 1781, and the British surrendered West Florida to Spain the same year. As part of the final agreement ending the American Revolution, Spain regained the rest of Florida in 1783. Having lost the thirteen colonies, England had little interest in colonial Florida after the war. The territory was isolated, and it had never produced large profits for England.

THE SECOND SPANISH PERIOD

Spain's return to Florida proved to be something less than a triumph. Spain had less power and influence in the Florida of the 1780s than it had had in the Florida it abandoned in 1763. English-speaking settlers who had come from Georgia and the Carolinas outnumbered Spanish-speaking settlers. The Spanish feared American expansion and they did not trust the British, whose influence in Florida was still considerable. Conflicts among all parties with interests in north Florida—the British, Americans, Spaniards, Indians, runaway slaves—were frequent.

In 1803 United States President Thomas Jefferson purchased the Louisiana Territory from France. A huge tract of land west and northwest of Florida, it left the United States in possession of the entire Southeast—except Florida. Spain knew it was just a matter

In 1813, American militiamen retaliated against Creek Indians who had attacked and killed several hundred settlers at Fort Mims in Alabama (left). General Andrew Jackson used the Fort Mims Massacre as a pretext for advancing toward Florida, where he intended to drive the British and their Indian allies out of Pensacola.

of time before the new United States would put pressure on to acquire Florida. The American military tried to accelerate the process by halfheartedly backing a revolution against Spain by American settlers in East Florida in 1812. The scheme failed, however, when the rebellion faltered and the American government withdrew its support.

During the War of 1812 between the United States and England, sentiment for the occupation of Florida by American soldiers was strong. American military commanders feared that if they did not occupy St. Augustine and Pensacola, England would. Congress did not support invading what was, in effect, a foreign country. Nevertheless, American troops, without congressional authorization, periodically marched into Florida to fight both Indians and the British. The most important of these raids occurred in November 1814, when General Andrew Jackson, known as "Old Hickory" for his forceful ways, marched into Pensacola. This was Spanish territory, but the Spaniards, unable to defend the town, had let the British occupy it. Moving on his own authority, Jackson drove the British and their Indian allies out of Pensacola. He continued to move west and defeated the British at New Orleans in the climactic battle of the War of 1812.

Andrew Jackson at Pensacola in 1818, when he returned to Florida to "punish" the Seminole Indians in what became known as the First Seminole War

Jackson figured prominently in Florida history during the next several years. He became the "enforcer" of United States policy. The United States clearly wanted Florida but could not justify taking it. The lawlessness of the north Florida frontier, however, helped the United States put pressure on Spain to give Florida up. The border country had become home to many Indians and runaway slaves, who used Florida as a base from which to raid settlements, farms, and plantations in Alabama, Georgia, and even the Carolinas. Life was hazardous for everyone, and when American settlers complained, Congress lent a sympathetic ear. The United States, in effect, told Spain either to police the territory or give it up.

In 1818, in what became known as the First Seminole War, Jackson's forces invaded Florida to fight the Seminole, who had been attacking American settlers. Charging Spanish officials with aiding the Indians, Jackson captured Pensacola, hoping to wrest

Florida from Spain. He defeated the Seminole, but his unauthorized seizure of Pensacola succeeded only in making Spain furious and his own government embarrassed. He also stirred British protests when he hanged two British traders who, he claimed, were assisting the Seminole.

FLORIDA BECOMES AMERICAN

Florida had become a refuge for runaway slaves, pirates, convicts, foreign adventurers, and hostile Indians. Spain could not control the region, nor could it keep forces hostile to the United States from using Pensacola and other ports. In 1819, Spain gave up. President James Monroe announced the Adams-Onis Treaty, deeding East and West Florida to the United States, on February 22, 1821.

Florida's two capitals, Pensacola and St. Augustine, lay about 400 miles (644 kilometers) apart. There were no roads between them. The fastest route from one town to the other was around the peninsula by sea, a trip that took from fifteen to twenty days. The territory quickly decided that its capital needed to be on middle ground. Tallahassee, once an Indian settlement, was chosen because of its central location. It was formally made the capital on March 4, 1824.

For the United States, Florida was a bargain. The government paid about $5 million to American settlers who had claims against Spain for various damages. It paid nothing to Spain directly. General Jackson returned—legally this time—as the military governor. Stated President Monroe, "to the acquisition of Florida too much importance cannot be attached."

The new territory arrived at a bargain price. The next few years were to be far more costly.

THE FRONTIER AND BEYOND

"They seem to be free from want or desire, no cruel enemy to dread; nothing to give them disquietude but the gradual encroachment of white people." Such was naturalist and adventurer William Bartram's description of the Seminole in the late 1700s. By 1822, however, the advancement of whites into Indian land was no longer "gradual."

THE SECOND SEMINOLE WAR

A new group of Indians had begun to arrive in Florida in the early eighteenth century. Most of them were Creeks from elsewhere in the Southeast. As their homelands had come increasingly under white domination, they welcomed the chance to immigrate to Florida. Florida was sparsely settled by whites, and its original Indian inhabitants had virtually disappeared after years of warfare, slave trading, and disease.

The new Indians in Florida became known as the Seminole, possibly from the Spanish *cimarron*, which means "wild and unruly," or from the Creek word *simanóle*, which means "runaways" or "those who separate." The Seminole occupied some of the finest, most fertile land in north Florida. For the most part, they lived in harmony with the Spanish and English governments of the eighteenth and early nineteenth centuries. But when thousands of American settlers arrived after the United States takeover, conflicts began. The white Americans wanted the

The Second Seminole War was touched off in 1835 when a group of Seminole warriors, angered at being forced by the American government to give up their land, attacked Major Francis Langhorne Dade and his troops near Bushnell, Florida.

Indians' rich farmland. They also were afraid that the Seminole, whose ranks included a number of former slaves, would lure their plantation slaves to freedom.

American policy became one of eviction. In 1830, Congress passed a removal act ordering eastern and southern Indians to relocate to western prairie lands. Some of the approximately five thousand Seminole living in Florida at that time agreed to uproot. Others, such as the great Seminole leader Osceola, stayed and fought to protect their land and culture.

The Second Seminole War began when the Seminole ambushed Major Francis Langhorne Dade and 110 American soldiers on December 28, 1835, near Bushnell, Florida. Only three of Dade's party survived, and the episode became known as the Dade Massacre. Although few large-scale battles followed, the Dade episode triggered seven years of bloody and expensive conflict. For the United States government, the war became a series of skirmishes. The Indians struck guerrilla-style, then melted into the pines and swamplands.

In 1837, while supposedly conferring under a flag of truce,

Osceola and eighty-one of his men were treacherously seized by General Thomas Sidney Jessup. Weakened by malaria, Osceola died a prisoner at Fort Moultrie, South Carolina, in 1838.

Osceola's death did not dampen the Seminole's will to fight. Their purpose was not to overcome the United States Army. They wanted merely to be left alone. However, Andrew Jackson had said, "I tell you that you must go and that you will go." Some bands, faced with starvation and weary of war, gave up. Said one chief: "I have been hunted like a wolf and now I am sent away like a dog." Jessup surrounded and captured four hundred Seminole who had shown up for the promise of truce talks.

The Second Seminole War never officially ended. The great majority of Seminole were forced to move westward or were killed. A remaining few hundred drifted into the swamps of south Florida as the army declared the war over. The United States never actually signed a peace treaty with the Seminole Nation.

The Second Seminole War had cost the lives of as many as two thousand American soldiers. Only one-fourth of these men died in action. Most died from disease, such as yellow fever, malaria, and dysentery. No one knows how many Seminole died, but by 1843, the government had shipped 3,824 to reservation lands in Oklahoma.

THE TWENTY-SEVENTH STATE

Florida was ready for statehood when it prepared a constitution in 1839. But Florida and its fifty-four thousand residents, nearly half of them black, could not enter the Union as a slave state without the addition of a matching free state to retain a balance in the Senate. When Florida was admitted to the Union on March 3, 1845, as a slaveholding state, Iowa was admitted as a free state.

By 1850, Florida had grown to a population of 87,445. Among the state's residents were 39,000 slaves and 1,000 free black people known as *freedmen*. The plantation economy, which had begun when the English occupied Florida in the eighteenth century, was in full operation in North Florida. The state's population and wealth were concentrated in north-central Florida, where the so-called plantation counties were. Yet the new state was expanding. Pioneer sugarcane planters such as Major Robert Gamble moved into Manatee County, not far from where Hernando De Soto had landed in 1539. Whites moving into the Big Cypress Swamp, Florida's last Indian refuge, touched off a three-year struggle in 1855 that became known as the Third Seminole War. Wanting to rid the area of Indians once and for all, the government posted rewards of up to $500 for live Indians. The fighting ended in November 1857, when a large army force discovered the Seminole's camp and Chief Billy Bowlegs surrendered. Most of the few Seminole remaining in Florida were paid by the government to go West. The rest retreated deeper into the swamps and were not pursued.

Cotton became the state's chief cash crop in those pre-Civil War days. The big plantation owners and planters became the state's social and political leaders. Since the plantations were dependent on slave labor, the owners took a dim view of any threat to the institution of slavery. A man's wealth was measured in Florida by the number of slaves he kept. Rumblings from Washington, D.C. and the North about abolition (the elimination of slavery) were not well-received by the planters. They felt that the government had no right to tell an individual how to run his own plantation.

Despite their political influence, the owners of big plantations were a small minority of the population. More typical of the new state were farmers with few or no slaves. These farmers usually lived in log cabins with tall chimneys and huge fireplaces. They wore clothes made at home and slept on mattresses filled with straw or Spanish moss. A family that improved its lot might build a frame house with porches on three sides. The Indians had been removed, and the Yankees and abolitionists were still up North. For white Floridians, it was a brief interlude of prosperity.

THE SLAVERY ISSUE

For black Floridians, life was not nearly as rosy. The institution of slavery was a matter of great debate in the nation. As slaveholders in Florida became more concerned about the future of slavery, they became more watchful of their "property." The few hundred freedmen were especially worrisome. Many whites looked upon them as potential sources of rebellion. By 1845, it was illegal in Florida for slave owners to free their slaves unless they also assisted them in leaving the state. Other laws of the 1840s and 1850s made Florida freedmen subject to discriminatory practices. But white arrogance was probably best illustrated by an 1858 Florida statute. It allowed free people of African descent to select a master of their choice and become slaves! The court records of Escambia County show that two persons, both of mixed black and white parentage, elected in 1861 to become slaves. No details of the circumstances surrounding their curious choice are provided.

The Spanish in Florida had been relatively fair to former slaves. The custom continued in St. Augustine and Pensacola, the old Spanish towns, even under American rule. Freedmen owned property and businesses and served on juries with whites.

Florida's slaves normally attended "white" churches, most of which were Baptist, Methodist, Episcopalian, or Presbyterian. But they had to sit in "reserved" sections, and they often had to listen to pastors who supported slavery and the right of secession.

The right of a state to leave the Union was an issue that Floridians heard about often in the late 1850s. Most, though not all, supported this idea, and many no doubt realized that secession was going to happen. But they probably were not aware of how far-reaching the consequences would be.

SECESSION

In January 1861, Richard Keith Call stood on his Tallahassee doorstep confronted by a rowdy group of secessionists. Call was a former territorial governor of Florida, a commander during the Seminole War, a loyal Floridian, and a slaveholder. He was also a Unionist. In other words, like many Floridians, he was against secession. But a special convention had just drawn up a statement of secession. Now the secessionists mocked Call, who responded, "Well, gentlemen, all I wish to say to you is that you have just opened the gates of Hell."

The Southern states, led by South Carolina, had known that secession and war with the North could come. President Abraham Lincoln and the Republicans had made it clear they opposed the right of individual states to secede from the Union. Lincoln foresaw the end of slavery in the United States, and had several ideas about how to accomplish that end. Southerners championed not only the continuation of slavery, but the right to secede, if necessary, to maintain their way of life. Florida seceded on January 10, 1861. As many as fifteen thousand Floridians eventually served in the Confederate army during the Civil War, which lasted from 1861 to 1865. Another twelve hundred whites and nearly one thousand blacks served in the Union army.

An 1861 photo showing a Confederate camp near Pensacola

FLORIDA IN THE CIVIL WAR

Despite the fiery leadership of Governor John Milton, a die-hard Confederate, Florida did not play a crucial role in Civil War fighting. Its long coastline was virtually impossible to defend. Union troops immediately occupied some of the state's key ports: Fort Jefferson on the Dry Tortugas west of the Florida Keys, Fort Taylor on Key West, Fort Pickens outside Pensacola, and the old Spanish Castillo de San Marcos in St. Augustine. Union forces occupied Jacksonville four different times. Florida troops served outside their state, but the Confederate command had few troops for the defense of Florida.

Florida's chief role in the war was as a food producer for Southern armies. Florida supplied beef, and salt boiled from seawater. The salt, which was needed to preserve meat, sold for as much as one dollar per pound.

Many of Florida's poor, rural whites preferred to have nothing to do with the war. They had no slaves and did not want any trouble from either side. The few Unionists in the state kept a low profile, except in coastal towns such as Fernandina and Key West, which were occupied by Union troops.

People became resourceful as the war dragged on and goods became difficult to obtain. They made soap from fats and ashes, and shoes from deer and alligator skins. Many of the plantations, with the male owners at war, were operated by women and hired overseers.

The only major battle in Florida during the Civil War was fought at Olustee near Lake City on February 20, 1864. About five thousand Union soldiers marched inland from Jacksonville, hoping to recruit blacks, cut the Confederate supply line, gather cotton and lumber, and eventually take Tallahassee. A dug-in force of about five thousand Confederates stopped the Yankees, who retreated back to the coast. Between the two armies, 2,757 soldiers were either killed, wounded, captured, or missing. The Union suffered most of the casualties. The battle kept Confederate lines open for another year, and the Union never mounted another large-scale invasion of interior Florida.

RECONSTRUCTION

The Union finally occupied Tallahassee on May 10, 1865. The painful process of putting the broken South back together had begun. The process was called Reconstruction, and it was to last for several years.

Florida expected to rejoin the Union quickly, but the United States would not readmit states until they guaranteed voting rights to blacks. Florida's provisional government had prohibited black voting rights. Furthermore, it enacted a series of Black Codes, laws that applied only to blacks. Eventually, Florida moderated its laws and implemented a constitution that was

During Reconstruction, when Florida was under federal military rule, United States troops (background) were stationed near the state capitol in Tallahassee.

acceptable to the federal government. It also ratified the fourteenth amendment to the United States Constitution, giving blacks some basic rights. On July 25, 1868, Florida was readmitted to the United States, and its elected representatives were given their proper places in Congress.

Many problems existed at home. Violence and lawlessness, often related to tension between blacks and whites, were common. The secretive Ku Klux Klan began terrorizing blacks. Northerners poured into Florida. Some, called carpetbaggers, were looking for easy money by investing in cheap land and labor. Others were federal employees, sent to insure that laws, especially those covering the rights of blacks, were being observed.

During Reconstruction, most of the large number of Northerners and new black voters were Republicans. Though Florida Democrats remained influential in the state legislature, Republicans dominated the Florida governorship until 1876. In 1877, the last federal troops left Florida, and the state's white Democrats began to reassert their traditional political strength. The state had begun to curb the Klan, and memories of the war had begun to fade. Northerners began to visit Florida for pleasure rather than strictly for politics or profit.

The docks at Pensacola bustled with activity in the 1880s, when Florida began to develop rapidly as a result of the building of railroads, new land development, the growing citrus and tobacco industries, and the discovery of phosphate.

POSTWAR PROSPERITY

After the war, the state and its developers began to create the image of a state with far more to offer than cotton. The building of railroads, the discovery of phosphate, the growing citrus industry, and a tremendous surge in population put Florida in an upward spiral. Between 1880 and 1900, Florida's population grew from 296,493 to 523,542.

Three men, Yankees all, played key roles in Florida's emergence from the long shadow of cotton: Hamilton Disston, Henry Plant, and Henry Flagler. Disston, from Philadelphia, demonstrated that vast tracts of south Florida swamp could be drained and then used for farming or building. Plant and Flagler, both originally from Connecticut, became involved in railroads, commerce, and tourism.

Flagler had made a personal fortune as a partner of John D. Rockefeller in Standard Oil. While vacationing in St. Augustine during the winter of 1883-84, he decided to move to Florida and begin a second career. A man of foresight as well as wealth, Flagler built an extensive railroad and hotel empire along the east coast of Florida. By 1896, his Florida East Coast Railroad had reached Miami. At the same time, the Intracoastal Waterway was being constructed. Dredging began in 1883, and by 1912 a small boat could travel slightly inland all the way from Fernandina Beach, near Florida's northern border, to the Keys.

Henry B. Plant was a spender, and, like Flagler, a man with big ideas. He built major hotels, founded a line of steamships, developed the port of Tampa for shipping, and built hundreds of miles of railroad on Florida's west coast.

No place in the state was more alive than Tampa. The discovery of phosphate deposits in Tampa in 1883 began one of the state's greatest industries. In 1886, thousands of workers flocked to new cigar factories in Tampa. Telegraph lines appeared in 1884, a street railway system in 1885, and electricity in 1887. The Plant Railway built docking facilities at Port Tampa in 1888. Telephone service began in 1890, and the Florida Central and Peninsula Railroad reached the city in the same year.

Tampa had become the world's cigar capital. The new Florida railroads were being followed by tourists, agriculture, and new industry. North Florida citrus growers began to move south after a disastrous freeze during the winter of 1894-95, developing more and more of Florida as they went.

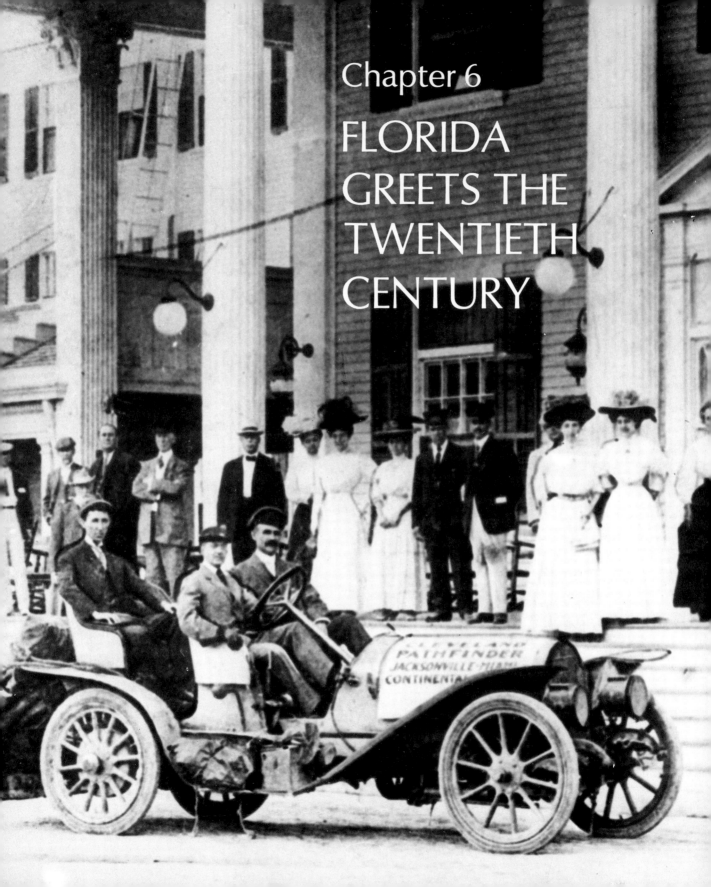

Chapter 6

FLORIDA GREETS THE TWENTIETH CENTURY

FLORIDA GREETS THE TWENTIETH CENTURY

"White man arrived here relatively late, but he arrived well-equipped and mechanized to challenge nature," University of Miami Professor Ronald Hofstetter once observed. As the twentieth century began, people did not win all their challenges to nature in the Sunshine State, but they rapidly gained the advantage.

THE EARLY TWENTIETH CENTURY

Around the turn of the century, Florida drained thousands of acres of swampland in the southeast. Land speculators, people hoping to make money on land sales, poured in. Henry Flagler built a railroad to Homestead, southwest of Miami in the heart of reclaimed agricultural land. Flagler also took on what seemed like a farfetched scheme: a railroad linking the Florida Keys all the way to Key West. In 1912, "Flagler's Folly," as it was called, was finished. Key West was linked to the mainland.

The mainland railroads shipped tons of Florida citrus north and carried thousands of tourists south. Those who did not ride the trains showed up in cars. And in a preview of an era still ahead, the nation's first regularly scheduled airline flight took place between Tampa and St. Petersburg on January 11, 1914.

Despite the continuing influx of northerners into the state, remnants of the old southern attitudes could still be found in

Florida. The election of Sidney J. Catts to the governorship in 1916 was a case in point. In campaign speeches, Catts attacked blacks, Catholics, and conservation measures. Catts's methods and speeches fanned the embers of bigotry in a state that had previously showed some religious tolerance. Florida had elected David Levy Yulee, America's first Jewish senator, in 1845. And in 1902, Stephen Mallory II, a Catholic, had won renomination for one of Florida's United States Senate seats by the state's overwhelmingly Protestant population.

Though compulsory school attendance became law during Catts's term of office, he did little to improve Florida's image. But events just around the corner would do so — at least for a while.

BOOM AND BUST

The Roaring Twenties were years of national prosperity, change, and a new sense of freedom. Nowhere were the twenties more "roaring" than in southern Florida. In the early 1920s one could spot two elephants, Carl and Rosie, pulling cartloads of kids around Miami Beach. It was all part of Carl Fisher's pitch to sell land to the children's parents. In the twenties, everyone in south Florida was selling land, it seemed. Fisher was one of the most successful at the trade.

Fisher had founded the Prestolite Company and the Indianapolis Speedway in Indiana. He incorporated his newest project, Miami Beach, in 1915. Development of Miami Beach had been initiated by John S. Collins, a New Jerseyan who originally had wanted to start a coconut plantation there. Soon Fisher began an advertising campaign unlike any seen before. American humorist Will Rogers once said that Fisher "rehearsed the mosquitoes till they wouldn't bite you until after you'd bought."

Flagler Street in downtown Miami as it looked in 1920, just before the Florida real-estate boom began

Fisher was not alone in his development plans. George Merrick developed Coral Gables, a glitzy suburb of Miami. Merrick's own fleet of buses brought potential buyers into Coral Gables. He even hired famous politician and orator William Jennings Bryan to praise the Miami area. Bryan was paid $50,000 per year to call Miami the "only city in the world where you can tell a lie at breakfast that will come true by evening."

A land rush was underway by 1924. Many people returned to Florida after having been stationed there as soldiers during the Spanish-American War or World War I. Others were simply tired of northern urban life. Meanwhile, the automobile was gaining popularity and the new Dixie Highway made Florida easier to reach from the Midwest. The nation as a whole was prospering, and people had money for travel and for land investment. Florida land seemed an especially good investment. Best of all, there were no state income or inheritance taxes.

In the summer of 1925, two men paid $3 million for a stretch of beachfront property north of Miami Beach. Two days later they sold it for more than $7.5 million. A week later, the same beach

Two legacies of the wealth that came to Florida's east coast in the early twentieth century are Coral Gables' Venetian Pool (left), created as part of the elegant planned community built by George Merrick in the 1920s; and the Breakers (above), Henry Flagler's famous Palm Beach hotel.

brought $42 million! A New York bank clerk took $1,000 to Florida and returned home three weeks later with $375,000. These and other stories of people achieving instant wealth by buying and selling Florida property prompted a speculative boom.

No one seemed to notice or care at first, but more lots than available land were being sold. As someone said, if all the lots sold were actually built upon, they would house the entire eastern half of the nation. Outsiders began to question the sales, and doubts about the wisdom of buying land in Florida began to spread. In August 1925, the Florida East Coast Railroad had to slow operations for major track repairs, slowing the supply of building materials from the north. When builders turned to ships to bring in materials, a ship capsized and blocked the harbor in Miami. By 1926, sales had slowed, and land prices had fallen drastically. The final blow came when a hurricane ripped into Miami on September 19, 1926. In south Florida, 392 people died and 6,281 were injured. Another deadly hurricane in 1928 killed at least 1,800 people in south Florida; only the Galveston and Johnstown floods had drowned more people. The boom was over.

Though it didn't last, the Florida boom had helped Miami become a major city. Its population had risen from 29,571 in 1920 to 110,637 by 1930. But in 1929, just as Florida was beginning to recover, the stock market crashed. Florida, like the rest of the nation, plunged into a depression.

DEPRESSION AND WAR

The Great Depression of the 1930s slowed Florida's economic growth even more. By 1934, almost one-fourth of the state's residents were receiving public aid. Tourism dwindled, of course. Yet Florida's population grew 29 percent during the decade, bringing it up to nearly 1.9 million residents by 1940.

World War II brought the Great Depression to an end. It also brought a new surge of people and energy to the Sunshine State. Florida was ideal for military training because of its year-round good weather and flat terrain. It was particularly useful for pilot training. By war's end in 1945, Florida had forty military air bases.

Tourism was disrupted during the war. Hotels were converted to barracks, training schools, and even hospitals. Florida is the closest mainland location to the Panama Canal, which made it a very important military site. The beaches were patrolled by military aircraft, the Civil Air Patrol, autos, cavalry, and blimps. Most of the coast-watching was designed to spot German submarines, which occasionally torpedoed United States ships within sight of the coast early in the war.

One of the most bizarre incidents of war on the home front had Florida connections. On the night of June 18, 1942, four men stood on the sands of Ponte Vedra Beach. From their dress and identification papers, they might have been American tourists. But if so, they would have been the first tourists to arrive in Florida by

Four German spies, shown here during their trial, landed by submarine on the Florida coast in 1942.

German submarine. Edward Kerling, Herbert Haupt, Hermann Neubauer, and Werner Thiel were German spies. They landed undetected and buried explosives in the sand for later use. They took a bus to Jacksonville, split up, and traveled north. Betrayed by two other members of their group who had landed on Long Island, New York, they were arrested by the FBI. On August 8, 1942, they were executed in Washington, D.C.

After the war, Florida prospered. The population ballooned by 46 percent between 1940 and 1950. Many soldiers who had been stationed there during World War II came back as residents. The stage was set for even more dramatic growth and development.

INTO THE SPACE AGE

The state's population growth between 1950 and 1960 was a phenomenal 78.7 percent, bringing the population up to nearly 5 million. Additional highways and the growing use of air travel brought more tourists. Air conditioning helped, too. The state spent huge sums cultivating its sunny, windblown image.

Cape Canaveral, site of the John F. Kennedy Space Center, opened in 1950 as a missile-testing station. This 1973 photo shows the launching of the fourth crew of astronauts to visit Skylab, the first United States space station.

But Florida proved to be its own best commercial; many tourists came back to stay. Some vacationers just never left. Many new Floridians came to escape unfriendly governments. Cubans arrived by the thousands in the 1960s and again in 1980. Haitians flooded into Florida in the late 1970s and early 1980s to escape poverty and dictatorship at home.

Meanwhile, Florida was beginning to conserve its natural resources. In the late 1960s, Governor Kirk's administration helped close the door on a proposed Everglades jetport. Kirk's successor, Governor Reubin Askew, supported many conservation laws helping to protect wilderness and wetlands from unchecked development. In the 1980s, Governor Bob Graham began costly long-term projects to restore the Everglades and protect coastal habitats.

Florida also began to take stock of its industrial assets. With its cattle, vegetable, and citrus markets well established, Florida encouraged industrial expansion. Jobs opened in many new fields from electronics to space technology. The Kennedy Space Center at Cape Canaveral became a symbol of the state's new, modern role.

Cape Canaveral, at the midpoint of Florida's Atlantic coast, opened as a missile-testing station on July 24, 1950. A hybrid rocket composed of an American stage launched by a German V-2 missile lifted off with the earthshaking rumble that was to become a familiar sound at the Cape. Nearby Brevard County rumbled with activity, too. The population there increased almost fourfold between 1950 and 1960.

The National Aeronautics and Space Administration (NASA) began work at the Cape in 1958. The site and its program became increasingly important during President John F. Kennedy's administration. On August 25, 1961, President Kennedy announced that NASA's energies would be directed toward putting a man on the moon before the end of the decade. In 1963, NASA acquired 88,000 acres (35,614 hectares) for a major space-industries complex on Merritt Island, adjacent to the Cape. After the president's death, the space complex became known as the Kennedy Space Center. In 1969, NASA achieved President Kennedy's goal, as the world watched Neil Armstrong step onto lunar soil and announce, "That's one small step for a man, one giant leap for mankind."

NASA achieved such a record of success at the space center that the public was shocked when the space shuttle Challenger exploded in flight on January 28, 1986, shortly after launch from Cape Canaveral. The entire crew of seven died in the accident.

NASA has certainly had a major impact on the Florida economy — but so has Mickey Mouse. Mickey, of course, is the best-known symbol of Walt Disney World in Lake Buena Vista near Orlando. Disney World opened in October 1971, and central Florida has never been the same. Walt Disney himself picked the site in 1963. His associates bought more than 28,000 acres (11,332 hectares) of land for the project. The Magic Kingdom,

The phenomenal success of Disney World (left), which opened in 1971, has contributed to Florida's economic growth. EPCOT Center, which explores both the world of the future and the customs of countries around the world (above), was added to the Disney World complex in 1982.

with its family brand of fun, was an instant success. In 1982 another phase of the project, EPCOT (Experimental Prototype Community of Tomorrow) opened with a multinational theme. Almost 23 million people had visited EPCOT by the end of its first year of operation.

The success of such enterprises as Disney World and the Kennedy Space Center complex has stimulated Florida's growth. It was estimated in 1987 that Florida's population had grown 23 percent since 1980, moving the state's ranking up from seventh-most populous state in the country to fourth-most

In 1963, outside a governors conference being held in Miami, members of the Congress of Racial Equality (CORE) picketed against segregation and racial inequality.

populous state. The rising population has been accompanied by common growth-related problems. Managing natural resources—land and water—has been an issue of tremendous concern and importance. Another matter of concern is growing violence, particularly in the cities, and drug trafficking. A grand jury in 1982 reported that 75 percent of the marijuana and cocaine entering the United States was coming through southern Florida. Another report showed that violent crime in Dade County (Miami) had doubled in a relatively short time.

THE LONG ROAD TO INTEGRATION

Even when the state was achieving great strides economically after World War II, Florida's black people were rarely beneficiaries of the good. Segregation of the races had always been custom and law in Florida, as it was throughout the South. Restaurants, buses, hotels, public buildings, and schools were segregated. Florida's black population remained poorly educated and impoverished.

In 1954 the United States Supreme Court outlawed school segregation. The southern states, Florida included, did not rush to integrate schools, or any public places. Black people had to demonstrate for the right to eat at the same lunch counters as whites and to sit anywhere they chose on public buses. Florida managed to avoid many of the violent clashes that other states suffered, but there were major boycotts and demonstrations in Tallahassee in 1956, Daytona Beach and Jacksonville in 1963, and St. Augustine in 1964.

Governor LeRoy Collins walked a narrow line between the opposing wishes of blacks and many whites. He said there would be no integration in Florida schools "so long as it is not wise in the true light of the . . . facts of life as they exist . . . in our state." But Collins admitted that "our attitude generally in the past has been obstructive all along the line." Collins received backing from the black community when he argued that "We can find wise solutions if the white citizens will face up to the fact that the Negro does not now have equal opportunities."

Slowly, integration became reality as well as law. By the early 1970s, all of Florida's public schools were integrated. In the 1970s, Governor Askew became the first Florida governor to appoint significant numbers of blacks to important state positions.

But relations between Florida's black and white communities often smoldered. Rioting erupted in the Liberty City section of Miami in June 1980. Eighteen people died. The rioting was sparked by the acquittal of four white policemen who had been accused of beating to death Arthur McDuffie, a black businessman. The rioting also reflected the frustration of blacks with the new wave of Cuban immigrants. Many feared that Cubans would take their jobs by agreeing to work for lower wages. Relations between the races were once again tested—and found wanting. It was apparent that racial harmony, a goal of most Floridians, black and white, was still a goal, not a fact of life.

Chapter 7

GOVERNMENT AND THE ECONOMY

GOVERNMENT AND THE ECONOMY

Florida's government is divided into three branches: legislative, executive, and judicial. It is essentially the same governmental system used in other states and on the national level.

The state legislature consists of a 40-member state senate and a 120-member house of representatives. Senators are elected to four-year terms. Members of the house serve two-year terms. The legislature passes laws and may propose amendments to Florida's constitution. Any such amendments must then be voted on by the public.

Executive power in Florida is shared by the governor and a seven-member cabinet, all of whom are elected to four-year terms. The cabinet includes the lieutenant governor, attorney general, commissioner of agriculture, comptroller, secretary of state, commissioner of education, and treasurer. Though the state constitution says that the governor has supreme executive power, in Florida's unusual arrangement many issues are settled by the cabinet. Former Florida Governor Fuller Warren once remarked that Florida's cabinet system "spreads the heat," because the governor does not have to bear total responsibility for unpopular decisions when facing the critical eye of the public.

The governor is elected to a four-year term and can serve no more than two terms in succession. Among the governor's responsibilities, according to the state constitution, are enforcing laws, recommending new laws to the legislature, and submitting the state budget.

The judicial branch interprets laws and tries court cases. It consists of a state supreme court, five district courts of appeal, twenty circuit courts, and a county court for each county, each with one or more judges.

Floridians traditionally vote Democratic. In the century following 1876, the state had only one Republican governor, Claude Kirk (1967-71), until Bob Martinez defeated his Democratic opponent to win a four-year term in 1986. However, in that same year, Floridians elected a new Democratic senator and all six of the Democratic candidates for the state cabinet. However, Republican presidential candidates carried Florida from 1952 through 1984, with two exceptions: Lyndon Johnson in 1964 and Jimmy Carter in 1976.

EDUCATION

Education is the state's largest expense. Of some $6.9 billion spent on education in 1985-86, $5.2 billion came from the state and federal governments. In 1985-86, Florida spent $3,731 on each public school student. Florida had 823,000 grade-school students and 736,000 secondary-school students in its 2,200 public schools. Another 208,000 students attended private schools.

Florida has some thirty fully accredited private and public universities and colleges. The state university system has nine schools. The largest is the University of Florida at Gainesville, with an enrollment of more than thirty thousand. Three other major state universities are Florida State University at Tallahassee, the University of South Florida at Tampa, and Florida A & M at Tallahassee. Two of the state's largest private institutions are the University of Miami, noted for its marine-biology program, and Jacksonville University.

74

Florida's largest
university is the
University of Florida
at Gainesville (left).
The University of Miami
at Coral Gables (above)
is the state's largest
private school.

In response to its growing population, Florida has sharply
expanded its educational system. The community-college system
begun in 1957 sought to provide post-high-school-level education
within commuting distance of 99 percent of the state's population.
In the 1960s, the state opened four new universities, several
private colleges, and thirteen community colleges. The state now
has about twenty-eight community colleges and has been a
national model for the development of community-college
systems elsewhere.

THE ECONOMY

Florida's state budget in the late 1980s exceeded $15 billion.
Nearly half of the state's income comes from its general revenue
fund, mostly the product of state sales taxes. Much of the rest of
Florida's money comes from the federal government and from a
state income tax on corporations, begun in 1971. Florida has no
individual state income tax.

Florida's economy has several components. But the state's

appeal to tourists is its most important economic asset. The nearly
40 million tourists who visit Florida each year spend a staggering
$22 billion. Tourism and associated service industries—hotels,
restaurants, entertainment facilities—provide 79 percent of the
state's gross annual product.

AGRICULTURE

Citrus fruit is the most important agricultural product in the
state. So it is not surprising that the state flower is the orange
blossom. Thirty-two of Florida's sixty-seven counties have
commercial groves producing oranges, grapefruit, and tangerines.
The largest citrus-producing counties are Polk, Lake, Orange,
St. Lucie, Indian River, and Hardee. The state produces about
75 percent of America's grapefruit, oranges, lemons, limes,
tangerines, and kumquats.

Florida has more than 70 million citrus trees on 50,000 acres
(20,235 hectares). The state's orange production varies with
winter severity. In mild winters, it has reached as much as 200
million boxes. Oranges are the state's leading cash crop, worth
over $1 billion a year.

Produce of many varieties is grown in Florida, much of it in the

Florida produces about 75 percent of the nation's oranges and grapefruit (left), and is a major producer of beef cattle (right).

reclaimed swamplands of south-central Florida. Nuts, primarily pecans and peanuts, are a major crop. The most valuable field crop in Florida is sugarcane. The state's produce list includes bananas, avocados, mangoes, papayas, strawberries, melons, soybeans, corn, cotton, oats, wheat, celery, and tomatoes. Nationally, Florida ranks first in producing foliage plants and second (after California) in producing flowers.

Ponce de León brought a small herd of Andalusian cattle to Florida in 1521. Long after that humble beginning, cattle ranching became important in Florida. Much of it is in the Kissimmee area, near Orlando. The state's broad, open prairies were natural pastures. Constant experimentation and cross-breeding have produced cattle that thrive in Florida's warm weather. Today the state is a major producer of both beef and dairy cattle.

The state has achieved growing recognition for its Thoroughbred horses. Many breeders, several of whom are located in the Ocala area, have discovered the advantages of the state's mild weather. Only Kentucky and California produce more Thoroughbreds than Florida.

Florida phosphate pits provide 86 percent of the phosphate rock used in the United States.

NATURAL RESOURCES

Forests cover half of Florida. Slash pines are the most valuable to the logging industry. Cypress was once important, but Florida's commercial-grade cypress forests were virtually logged out by 1955. Along with timber, Florida forests provide raw material for a thriving paper-products industry.

Beneath the forests and pastures of the Sunshine State are the largest phosphate deposits in the United States. Florida supplies 86 percent of the nation's phosphate rock, much of it used in fertilizers. Most of the huge phosphate pits are in west-central and north-central Florida. Mines in Gadsden and Marion counties yield fuller's earth, a clay used to filter petroleum. Petroleum itself is being pumped from wells in both north and south Florida. In the early 1980s, Florida was the country's tenth-ranked oil-producing state. Some offshore sites give promise of increasing the state's reserves and potential.

Another mineral, the whitish-colored coquina rock, was one of the most popular construction materials during Florida's boom days in the early twentieth century. It is a type of limestone composed of broken coral and sea shells.

With an annual catch of fish and shellfish valued at $170 million, Florida is a leading commercial-fishing state. About 60 percent of the American red snapper harvest comes from offshore Florida waters. Grouper, pompano, mullet, and mackerel are among the other important market fish. Shellfish—Florida lobster, shrimp, clams, oysters, scallops, and crabs—account for over half of the total fisheries income.

MANUFACTURING

The processing of citrus fruit is one of the state's most prosperous industries. More than 170 million gallons (644 million liters) of concentrated orange juice are produced each year. Almost all of the nation's frozen orange juice originates in Florida. Other major manufactured goods are electric and electronic equipment, transportation equipment, chemicals, paper goods, and cigars. These items are produced at manufacturing centers scattered throughout the state. Chief among them are Tampa, St. Petersburg, Orlando, Miami, Fort Lauderdale, and Jacksonville.

Florida is trying to attract new, "clean" industries. Some of the newcomers include aircraft, pharmaceutical, and medical-equipment manufacturers. Florida is also the country's third-largest producer of motion pictures.

TRANSPORTATION

Only 400 miles (644 kilometers) of railroad track ran through Florida during the Civil War. Now there are 6,566 miles (10,565 kilometers) of track. Fifteen railroads offer freight service throughout much of Florida. Amtrak passenger trains serve about twenty Florida cities and link the state's population centers to such cities as Washington, D.C., New York, and Chicago.

One of the remarkable, but questionable, accomplishments in

Florida railroad history was the completion of Henry Flagler's Overseas Railway to Key West in 1912. The construction spanned seven years and cost between five hundred and a thousand lives. Three hurricanes struck during construction. One observer of the railway grumbled that it was "carrying nothing to nowhere for nobody," but it operated until the hurricane of 1935 scuttled it. Rather than try to restore rail service, the bridges were converted to highway traffic and the Overseas Highway was created.

Florida has 97,000 miles (156,073 kilometers) of roads, two-thirds of them surfaced. Four Interstate highways reach across Florida's northern perimeter and stretch south to Naples on the west coast and Miami on the east. Interstate 75 from Naples to Fort Lauderdale incorporates what used to be Alligator Alley, a high-speed, two-lane highway. Perhaps the most spectacular section of Florida highway is the 15-mile (24-kilometer) Sunshine Skyway, one of the nation's longest highways completely over water. The Skyway, part of Interstate 275, links the Bradenton area with St. Petersburg.

A marvel of convenience and design, Tampa International is often cited by air passengers as the finest airport in the nation. Tampa, however, is only one of the more than five hundred designated airfields in Florida. The busiest are at Miami, Fort Lauderdale-Hollywood, Tampa, Orlando, and Jacksonville. Air traffic to and from Florida during the December-April tourist season is often intense.

Not everyone flies, drives, or rides a train to Florida. Some travel by boat on the Atlantic Intracoastal Waterway, a 1,200-mile (1,931-kilometer) system of rivers, bays, and canals. Boats also enter by way of the Gulf Intracoastal Waterway. Thousands of visitors also reach Florida at one or another of fifteen deep-water ports, which serve as entry points to Florida and the United States.

The famous Seven Mile Bridge, shown here as it crosses Pigeon Key, is part of the 106-mile-long Overseas Highway that runs from Key Largo to Key West.

COMMUNICATION

The first Florida periodical was the *East Florida Gazette*, established in St. Augustine in 1783. Florida now has about 250 newspapers of which about 60 are published daily. The oldest is Jacksonville's *Florida Times-Union*, established in 1864. Other major dailies include the *Fort Lauderdale News*, *Miami Herald*, *Miami News*, *Pensacola Journal*, *St. Petersburg Times*, *Orlando Sentinel-Star*, *Tampa Tribune*, and *Sarasota Tribune*. The Miami area has several Spanish-language newspapers, including *El Diario/La Prensa*.

Florida has 350 radio stations and 60 television stations. The state's first radio station, WQAM in Miami, began broadcasting in 1921. Television in Florida was inaugurated in 1949 by Miami's WTVJ-TV.

Chapter 8
ARTS AND LEISURE

ARTS AND LEISURE

People in Florida always seem to have time for recreation and leisure activities. Florida's beaches, warm climate, and other natural features make it ideal for outdoor enthusiasts. And in recent years, Floridians have began to discover the beauties and joys of the arts, some of them homegrown, some imported. As one young Florida theatergoer, tongue-in-cheek, told a northern visitor, "Hey! We ain't just beach bums and bikinis down here no more!"

OUTDOOR RECREATION

Because of the favorable climate, Floridians can participate in tennis, golf, softball, basketball, and water sports throughout the year. The seas and waterways are a boater's dream. Sailing regattas are popular in coastal cities. Canoeists have an excellent choice of streams—from dark, brooding rivers such as the Peace and Myakka, to the intricate tidal streams of Everglades National Park. Other favorite water-related sports include parasailing, surfing, windsurfing, snorkeling, and diving. Shell and fossil hunters comb Florida's beaches. Divers explore Florida's freshwater springs and submerged caves as well as coral reefs in the Keys. A few search out sunken Spanish galleons for their millions of dollars in treasure and artifacts.

Florida's fishing can be exceptional. Florida's freshwater lakes and streams provide bass, bluegills, and crappies. The St. Johns

Fishing (left) and snorkeling (right) are only two of the many water-related activities enjoyed by Floridians.

River and Lake Okeechobee enjoy national reputations for their bass fishing. Saltwater anglers surf cast from beaches, from the decks of oceangoing boats, and from the grassy bottoms of mangrove-lined bays.

Hunters in Florida find a variety of prey. Quail and turkey are favorite upland game. Duck hunting can be outstanding in marshes. Deer and feral pigs (domestic pigs that have become wild) are the most popular big game.

The state has an excellent network of hiking trails. The Florida Hiking Trail, when completed, will snake 1,300 miles (2,092 kilometers) through the middle of the state. Eight hundred miles (1,287 kilometers) were open by the mid-1980s.

For almost all forms of outdoor recreation, Florida's numerous parks and protected lands are superb. As author Gerald Grow wrote in *Florida Parks*, they are "the still healthy portions of the great Florida wilderness." Thanks to diligent voters and responsive politicians, Florida has more than ninety state parks, recreation areas, preserves, gardens, and special-feature sites

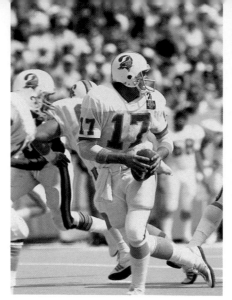

Florida has two National Football League teams: the Tampa Bay Buccaneers (left), and the Miami Dolphins. Each year, eighteen major-league baseball teams travel to Florida for spring training (right).

under state jurisdiction. The system, one of the most comprehensive in the nation, preserves examples of nearly every type of habitat in the state. The Florida Department of Natural Resources holds and maintains forests, beaches, marshes, lakes, islands, caverns, springs, sinkholes, rivers, and coral reefs.

County parks, city parks, and national land treasures such as Everglades National Park and the wilderness beaches of Canaveral National Seashore are scattered throughout Florida.

SPECTATOR SPORTS

Major-league baseball is one of the most popular spectator sports in Florida. Each spring, eighteen major-league teams travel down to Florida to begin spring training. In early April, all of the teams return home for the "real" season, but the few weeks of the "Grapefruit-League" season give thousands of Floridians a chance to enjoy their favorite team firsthand. Florida also fields the twelve-team Florida State League, a professional minor league.

Florida has two professional football teams. The Miami Dolphins, under coach Don Shula, entered the late 1980s as one of the most dominant teams in the National Football League. The team won the NFL's Super Bowl in 1973 and 1974, and its 17-0 record in 1972, including its playoff and 1973 Super Bowl victories, is an NFL record. The Tampa Bay Buccaneers, which joined the NFL as an expansion franchise in 1976, play in Tampa Stadium, a 72,126-seat facility. In their first decade, the Bucs had generally disappointing seasons.

Until the late 1980s, when a new stadium was constructed, the Dolphins played their home games in the 80,045-seat Orange Bowl. Each New Year's Day night, the Orange Bowl is the site of a major collegiate football game. The game is the highlight of a gala Orange-Bowl weekend in Miami. Two other major holiday football games are staged in Florida: the Gator Bowl contest in Jacksonville, and the Florida Citrus Bowl at Orlando.

The state fields four major collegiate football teams: the Florida State University Seminoles, the University of Florida Gators, the University of Miami Hurricanes, and the Florida A & M Rattlers. Many Florida colleges that do not have football—Jacksonville, Stetson, and the University of South Florida, for example—do have major basketball programs. Northern collegiate baseball teams flock to Florida in early spring to test their rusty skills against battle-ready Florida teams such as the University of Florida, Florida State, and Miami.

Soccer is a popular sport in Florida at all levels. Many high schools and colleges sponsor soccer teams, and the state has two professional teams: the Tampa Bay Rowdies and the Fort Lauderdale Strikers.

Jai alai is another important spectator sport in Florida. Jai alai is a version of handball played with long, narrow baskets that fit over the players' hands. Spectators at the *fronton* (stadium) wager on the outcome. Jai alai originated in the Basque regions of France and Spain, but later spread to other nations.

Greyhound racing draws 10 million spectators in Florida each year. In the early 1900s, the dogs chased a live rabbit. Now they race after a mechanical rabbit treated to smell like a real rabbit. Derby Lane in St. Petersburg is the largest track in Florida. Miami has three dog tracks. Horse racing also draws crowds in Florida. Hialeah Park in Hialeah and Gulfstream Park in Hallandale are the major Thoroughbred horse tracks. South Florida also has harness racing and quarter-horse racing at Pompano Park in Pompano Beach.

In the spring of 1987, basketball fans in Florida celebrated the announcement that two new teams would be added to the National Basketball Association: the Miami Heat, which would begin play during the 1988-89 season, and the Orlando Magic, which would begin play in 1989-90.

VISUAL AND PERFORMING ARTS

A state once faulted for its neglect of the arts, Florida has strived, as its publicists say, to become a "state *of* the arts." As recently as 1978, state money for arts programs totaled just $1.6 million. By 1985, the state was spending nearly $10 million on arts-related projects.

The John and Mable Ringling Museum of Art in Sarasota has an outstanding collection of Baroque art. Its collection of works by Peter Paul Rubens is one of the finest outside Europe. In St. Petersburg, the Museum of Fine Arts displays European, American, Far-Eastern, and pre-Columbian art. The Dali Museum displays the largest collection anywhere of works by controversial Spanish artist Salvador Dali. On the state's east coast, the Norton Gallery of Art in West Palm Beach is considered among the best small museums south of Washington, D.C.

The Ringling Museum of Art in Sarasota, built to resemble a fifteenth-century Florentine villa, houses the outstanding art collection of circus magnate John Ringling.

The best-known of Florida's theater groups is the Asolo State Theater in Sarasota. The state's oldest theater, Asolo has a professional training program in association with Florida State University. Other notable theaters are the Coconut Grove Playhouse in Miami and the Hippodrome Street Theater in Gainesville.

Music lovers enjoy such major symphonies as the Florida Orchestra, which plays in St. Petersburg, Tampa, and Clearwater; the Florida Symphony Orchestra of Orlando; the Jacksonville Symphony Orchestra; and the Philharmonic Orchestra of Florida in Fort Lauderdale. The state's foremost opera company, the Greater Miami Opera, is one of the nation's most respected companies. Dance enthusiasts enjoy the Gainesville Civic Ballet, the Florida Ballet of Jacksonville, and the Southern Ballet Theater in Winter Park.

ARCHITECTURE

The best way to appreciate Florida's many architectural traditions is to visit preserved and restored buildings and neighborhoods in several cities. Preservation efforts began in earnest in 1968 with the Governor's Conference on Historic Preservation.

In Pensacola, a fifty-block area known as the North Hill Preservation District features homes built in Classic Revival, Queen Anne, and Spanish Mission styles.

Key West produced its own distinctive style of architecture, a claim that few cities in the United States can make. Scores of what are known as Conch houses, many at least a hundred years old, can be found throughout Key West. (In the Keys, a "conch" is a native-born Key Wester). Conch houses are characterized by big verandas, shutters, ornate wooden railings, cisterns to catch rainwater, and long eaves and gutters. Small roof hatches called scuttles release hot air. Conch houses borrow from a number of architectural styles, including Early American New England, Bahamian British Colonial, and the French and Spanish-inspired buildings of New Orleans.

More-recent architecture of interest is Addison Mizner's work in Palm Beach and Boca Raton. Mizner was an eccentric architect who built ostentatious mansions for the very wealthy in the 1920s. One critic commented that Mizner's " 'boom-Spanish' designs made homes look like wedding cakes, heavy on the pink frosting and frills." Frank Lloyd Wright, one of America's greatest architects, felt differently; he called Mizner's architecture the work of a genius. Wright himself designed nine buildings on the campus of Florida Southern College in Lakeland.

The more than eight hundred buildings clustered around

Florida architecture ranges from the charming Conch houses of Key West (top left), to the streamlined 1930s buildings of Miami's Art Deco District (top and bottom right), to such opulent mansions as John Ringling's C'ad'zan (bottom left).

Flamingo Park that comprise Miami Beach's Art Deco District were the first twentieth-century buildings to be listed in the National Register of Historic Places. The buildings show a curious mixture of porthole windows, glass-block construction, ribbon windows, bands of pastel coloring, and other stylistic touches characteristic of south Florida in the 1920s and 1930s.

In nearby Coral Gables are George Merrick's Mediterranean designs of the 1920s. Other Merrick houses in Coral Gables have details that are reminiscent of buildings in China, France, and South Africa, places where Merrick had never been. Another architectural delight in Florida is circus magnate John Ringling's house, C'ad'zan ("House of John" in the Italian dialect of Venice), on Sarasota Bay. The thirty-room mansion was patterned after the Doges' Palace in Venice.

One of the newest architectural wonders in south Florida is Miami's Mediterranean-style Metro-Dade Cultural Center, designed by Philip Johnson.

LITERATURE

Florida's literary heritage is as old as European settlement in the New World. As far as is known, Florida's first "literature" was *Fontaneda's Memoir*, Domingo Escalante de Fontaneda's account of his seventeen years among the Calusa Indians in southern Florida. At the age of thirteen, de Fontaneda was en route from Cartagena (a Spanish outpost in Columbia) to Spain when he was shipwrecked in the Florida Keys. He was captured by the native Calusas, and lived with them until a Spanish expedition found him in 1562.

Most of the many resident and non-resident writers who followed de Fontaneda had less-trying experiences in Florida. An exception, however, was Stephen Crane. Crane was shipwrecked off Florida's east coast when the *Commodore* foundered in 1897. His experiences in a lifeboat became the basis for his classic short story "The Open Boat."

Crane was one of many well-known nineteenth-century American authors who came to Florida. John Muir, best known for his conservation activities on the Pacific coast and in the Far West, walked from Fernandina to Cedar Key in the mid-1850s. The experience became *A Thousand Mile Walk to the Gulf*. William Cullen Bryant and Georgia poet Sidney Lanier wrote poetry in and about Florida in the 1800s. Harriet Beecher Stowe, author of

Uncle Tom's Cabin, inspired a tourist boom along the St. Johns River with her inviting tales of tropical life in *Palmetto Leaves*.

Many prominent twentieth-century writers have worked in Florida. None has loomed as large as Illinois-born Ernest Hemingway. Hemingway wrote some of his finest novels, including *For Whom the Bell Tolls* and *A Farewell to Arms*, in Key West during the 1930s. His only novel with a Keys setting, however, was the less-acclaimed *To Have and Have Not*.

Marjorie Kinnan Rawlings is one of Florida's best-known resident writers. Rawlings lived in the rural scrub country near the Ocala National Forest. Her novel *The Yearling*, the bittersweet story of twelve-year old Jody Baxter and his pet deer, won the 1939 Pulitzer Prize. She also wrote the autobiographical *Cross Creek*, in which she expressed a sensitivity for Florida that no doubt many writers before and since have felt. "We need above all, I think, a certain remoteness from urban confusion," she wrote, "and while this can be found in other places, Cross Creek offers it with such beauty and grace that once entangled with it, no other place seems possible to us."

MacKinlay Kantor of Sarasota is best known for *Andersonville*, a fictionalized but accurate account of the notorious Confederate prison of the same name. Another Sarasotan, John D. MacDonald, wrote the best-seller *Condominium*, as well as dozens of popular mysteries featuring detective Travis McGee. Resident author Marjorie Stoneman Douglas is best remembered for her classic nonfiction book *The Everglades: River of Grass*. Perhaps better than anyone else, Douglas captured the pulse of south Florida's magnificent Everglades. "The whole system was like a set of scales on which the sun and the rains, the winds, the hurricanes, and the dewfalls, were balanced," she wrote, "so that the life of the vast grass and all its . . . forms were kept secure."

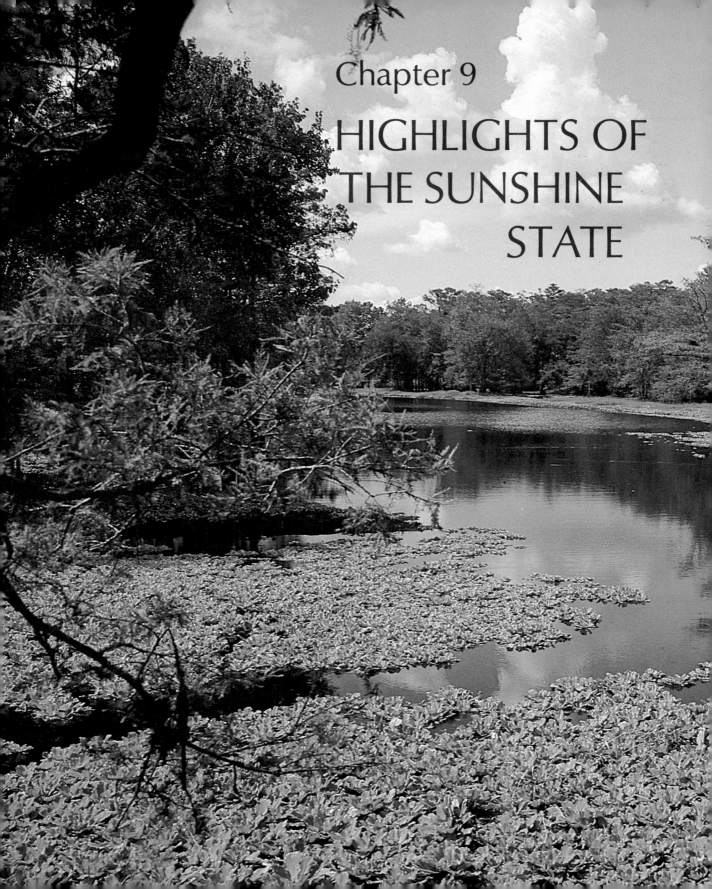

Chapter 9

HIGHLIGHTS OF THE SUNSHINE STATE

HIGHLIGHTS OF THE SUNSHINE STATE

If you drove along Florida's perimeter, striking inland here and there, you would drive more than eighteen hundred miles (nearly three thousand kilometers). But your effort would reveal the amazing diversity of people, natural beauty, and attractions in the Sunshine State.

THE NORTH

Pensacola, at the western end of the Florida panhandle, is a gold mine of history. The Pensacola Historic District features restored homes, galleries, shops, and museums. The Pensacola Naval Air Station, known as the "cradle of naval aviation," boasts the country's only Naval Aviation Museum. Nearby, Gulf Island National Seashore has some of the finest stretches of white sand in the state.

Two hundred miles (323 kilometers) eastward in north Florida is Tallahassee, the state capital. The new capitol, built in 1977, is here, as are the Florida State and Florida A & M campuses, the Civil War battlefield called Natural Bridge, and stately old plantation homes among the pines. Two outstanding natural attractions are Wakulla Springs and Maclay Gardens State Park. In the 1950s, the motion picture *The Creature from the Black Lagoon* was filmed in the strange and eerie environment of Wakulla Springs State Park.

Jacksonville, situated on the St. Johns River, is sometimes fondly referred to as "the working son in the Florida family of playboys."

The far northeastern coast of Florida is often called Florida's "first coast" because it was the first part of the state to be permanently settled. Jacksonville, situated on the St. Johns River, is 169 miles (272 kilometers) east of Tallahassee via Interstate 10. It is both Florida's largest city, with a population of about 550,000, and its most industrialized, sometimes called "the working son in the Florida family of playboys."

South of Jacksonville is St. Augustine, the nation's oldest city. Established in 1565 by Pedro Menéndez de Avilés, its restored streets, old buildings, horse-drawn carriages, and Castillo de San Marcos National Monument make it a favorite destination of history seekers. The St. Augustine Alligator Farm is one of the best of its kind. Tourists can walk a boardwalk within arm's reach of dozens of alligators and watch performances of 'gator-wrestling. Inland, along the St. Johns, is Palatka. According to old-timers, a person used to be able to walk across the river on the backs of alligators. Now, residents joke, the 'gators are gone, eaten by the largemouth bass.

One of Florida's earliest highways, A1A, runs all the way along the Atlantic coast. Along the route from St. Augustine to Daytona Beach are Marineland, the first of the world's oceanariums, and

Washington Oaks Garden, a wonderland of blossoms. Daytona itself is one of Florida's busiest cities. Each spring it is literally invaded by thousands of vacationing—or rampaging, according to some residents—college students. Some Daytona hotels post Welcome, Collegians! signs, perhaps as a peace offering.

Motorists can drive on the hard Daytona sand at a less-than-brisk ten miles (sixteen kilometers) per hour. Earlier in the century, thirteen auto speed records were set on Daytona sand. Now the Daytona International Speedway, well removed from the beach, hosts major professional auto races.

ORLANDO AND CENTRAL FLORIDA

A few miles south and west of Daytona are the theme parks of central Florida. The best known of these is Walt Disney World in Lake Buena Vista near Orlando. Adults obviously enjoy Disney World as much as do children. They outnumber youngsters four-to-one in admissions.

The success of Disney World prompted other theme parks, such as Orlando's Sea World. Sea World features water skiers, a glass tunnel that passes through a shark tank, and trained sea mammals. Its main attraction is a family of killer whales that perform in Shamu Stadium.

Orlando itself is a booming, modern metropolis. It has almost as many parks and lakes as hotel rooms. Ocala, north of Orlando, is noted for its many Thoroughbred horse farms. The sprawling Ocala National Forest and the hundreds of lakes in the area attract anglers, campers, and hikers.

East of Orlando, little more than a half-hour drive away, is the Kennedy Space Center at Cape Canaveral. Although Kennedy Spaceport occupies 140,000 acres (56,658 hectares), NASA uses

Tours of the
Kennedy Space Center
include a visit to
the gigantic Vehicle
Assembly Building.

only a small percentage of that land. The virtual wilderness of
marsh, woodland, and beach around the spaceport is public land:
the Merritt Island National Wildlife Refuge and the Canaveral
National Seashore. The seashore contains the longest strip of
undeveloped beach in Florida. White sand and gentle dunes
stretch for 25 miles (40 kilometers), making an ideal refuge for
nesting sea turtles, migrating birds, and human visitors.

The Spaceport Visitor Center traces the space program from
Explorer I, America's first satellite, to the space shuttle. The center
is the starting point for touring the huge Kennedy complex. A bus
carries visitors to the Vehicle Assembly Building, space shuttle
launch pads, and a Saturn V rocket. A Saturn V, made of 6 million
pounds (2.7 million kilograms) of steel, carried Neil Armstrong to
the moon from Cape Canaveral in 1969. Almost as imposing as
the rocket is the Vehicle Assembly Building, one of the biggest
buildings in the world. New York's Empire State Building could, if
chopped into sections, be stored in the VAB.

Laced with canals, rivers, and lagoons, Fort Lauderdale is a boater's delight.

MIAMI AND THE SOUTHEAST

After immersing oneself in the futuristic world of Kennedy Space Center, one can travel south to the state's most famous resort area, the fabled "Gold Coast." Here, giant hotels crowd the beaches and secluded mansions are hidden away behind stucco walls and coconut palms. Yachts bob in the harbors of exclusive clubs. Towns such as Jupiter Island and Palm Beach have some of the wealthiest residents in America.

Amid the Gold Coast communities is Fort Lauderdale. The original Fort Lauderdale was a wooden fort built during the Seminole War. Today's Fort Lauderdale sprang to life with the advent of Henry Flagler's railroad in 1911. Sometimes known as the Venice of America, Fort Lauderdale has 250 miles (402 kilometers) of lagoons, canals, and rivers; nearly 7 miles (11 kilometers) of Atlantic beachfront; and a deepwater port.

South of Fort Lauderdale is Miami—Florida's second-largest city, largest metropolitan area, and the hub of southeast Florida. Miami is a cosmopolitan city; Spanish seems to be spoken as much as English. Thousands of tourists and residents from overseas add an even greater assortment of tongues.

The centerpiece of Miami's large Cuban community is Little Havana. Calle Ocho (Southwest Eighth street), the main street, buzzes with the traffic of sidewalk cafes and boutiques. On sale are such local specialties as *ceviche*, raw fish in a lime marinade, and spirals of fried sweet dough called *churros*.

Miami is a major international banking-and-commerce center. Its business district is a showplace of high-rise glass-and-steel architecture. Mirror glass reflects the blue water of Biscayne Bay and streets lined with regal palms. A vibrant city, Miami claims to have the busiest port in the world.

In the Miami area are several attractions, including the Metro-Dade Cultural Center, which includes a library, a historical museum, and the Center for the Fine Arts; Fairchild Gardens, an eighty-three-acre (thirty-four-hectare) landscaped garden; Metrozoo, one of the nation's finest newer zoos; and Parrot Jungle, a delightful woodland splashed with the reds, blues, and greens of parrots and other exotic birds.

Across a narrow strip of water is world-famous Miami Beach, an island once described by author Polly Redford as a "billion-dollar sandbox." The "Beach," though still a pleasant vacation spot, is no longer considered, as it once was, the ultimate Florida resort. In the 1970s, Disney World and other, less crowded resorts lured tourists away from Miami Beach, and the city began to fall into disrepair. Today, however, attempts are being made to revitalize the area. Parks and beaches have been cleaned and improved, and plans for new development are underway.

THE FLORIDA KEYS

A few miles south of Miami, U.S. 1 crosses a bridge from the mainland to Key Largo, the first of thirty-two islands connected

A floating cottage off Key West, the southernmost town in the continental United States

by the 100-mile (161-kilometer) Overseas Highway. Another 850 Keys, many of them mere bits of exposed coral rock crowned by mangrove trees, lie unconnected by the road to Key West.

The Keys have a laid-back, sea-shack atmosphere. Most of them have been abused by wanton development. For a long time anything could be built anywhere in Monroe County, which encompasses the Florida Keys. Careful zoning was not considered when the Keys were first developed.

But if the islands themselves do not seem particularly special, the waters surrounding them are. The sparkling, blue-green water of the Keys is incredibly rich with fish, lobsters, and marine life in blazing color. The water is well worth a visit. At John Pennekamp Coral Reef State Park, one can go eye-to-eye with the fascinating undersea creatures of the reef.

Key West, the last stop, has resorts on its perimeter. But downtown Key West probably has not changed much since Ernest Hemingway's era half a century ago. Century-old Conch houses still line narrow streets. The subtropical greenery helps perpetuate an authentic, unkempt look. The town is certainly not like the plush resort towns on the Gold Coast; it has neither the sweeping beaches nor the wall-to-wall apartments and hotels. Its unaffected, leisurely atmosphere, its potpourri of inhabitants, and its

Fort Jefferson lies on Garden Key in the Dry Tortugas.

remoteness are reason enough for many visitors to drive the length of the Overseas Highway.

When the Florida peninsula was largely wilderness, Key West was a thriving town. Incorporated in 1828, Key West built an economy based on "wrecking," which depended on the misfortune of merchant shippers. Wreckers made their living by taking advantage of the many shipwrecks that occurred on the dangerous reefs. Piracy was once a steady occupation in the Keys as well, and Tavernier in the Upper Keys is named for one of the "brethren of the coast." Today treasure-hunting in the Keys is a serious venture. Professionals do their homework in painstaking detail, sometimes even traveling to Spain for a peek at dusty naval records.

About 68 miles (109 kilometers) west of Key West are the Dry Tortugas, a group of tiny coral keys accessible only by boat or seaplane. Ponce de León, who discovered the islands in 1513, named them the Tortugas because of the great number of tortoises living there. On Garden Key is massive Fort Jefferson, the largest brick fort in the Western Hemisphere. Begun in 1846, the fort was never completed. After the Civil War, it was used as a prison. Its most famous inmate was Dr. Samuel Mudd, who was unjustly convicted of conspiracy for giving John Wilkes Booth medical aid after Booth assassinated Abraham Lincoln.

THE GULF COAST

Back on the southern tip of the peninsula, near Homestead, one can take Route 27 to drive through Everglades National Park, the largest subtropical wilderness in the country. The road ends in the village of Flamingo, where visitors can look across the flats and islands of Florida Bay. Along the way, several interpretive exhibits explain the unique ecology of the national park. Trails lead to ponds and marshes where, in winter, large numbers of water birds assemble.

U.S. Route 41, the Tamiami Trail, travels north and west of the national park. It passes several Seminole villages and souvenir stands as it pushes from the Everglades to the Big Cypress National Preserve. The really massive bald cypress trees are almost gone, but there are plenty of small cypresses and islands of pine set in the wetlands.

Some of the most magnificent wild country in Florida is in the Fakahatchee Strand State Reserve. Part of the Big Cypress, the Fakahatchee has wild royal palms and forty-four species of native orchids. The Tamiami Trail and Florida Route 29 cut through the Fakahatchee. Route 29 also leads to Everglades City, the boaters' gateway to the north end of Everglades National Park.

Between sparkling Naples and Fort Myers is the National Audubon Society's Corkscrew Swamp Sanctuary. A boardwalk leads into a forest of giant bald cypresses. Some of the giant trees, anchored in a lush swamp, were growing there before Ponce de León's visit to Florida.

Thomas Edison's winter home and a museum displaying many of his inventions are open for public viewing in Fort Myers. Sanibel and its sister island Captiva lie offshore, connected to the mainland by a toll bridge. Both islands have exceptional seashells,

Tampa, Florida's third-largest city, is emerging as an important business and financial center.

and resorts in abundance. The J.N. "Ding" Darling National Wildlife Refuge on Sanibel is a haven for alligators and birds. On spring evenings, flocks of pink spoonbills fly across the sunset.

About fifty-five miles (eighty-eight kilometers) north of Fort Myers is Venice, an appealing seaside town with miles of dark-sand beach noted for its fossils. The winter quarters of the Ringling Brothers and Barnum and Bailey Circus are here. Sarasota, fifteen miles (twenty-four kilometers) north on U.S. 41, has long, white-sand beaches, a wealth of cultural institutions on its bay, and Myakka River State Park, a natural treasure, nearby.

North of Sarasota, in Bradenton, the De Soto National Memorial on the Manatee River estuary marks Hernando De Soto's supposed entry point in Florida in 1539. The nearby Sunshine Skyway whisks travelers across Tampa Bay to St. Petersburg. Another long bridge from St. Petersburg leads to the city of Tampa.

Busch Gardens in Tampa is one of Florida's premier tourist attractions. Covering 300 acres (121 hectares), it is a pulsating blend of thrill rides, floral displays, and animal exhibits. A monorail glides over a plain dotted with African animals, part of the attraction's Dark Continent theme. For those who want a more exciting ride, there is the Python, a twisting, lurching, roller-coaster.

Cypress Gardens (above), a lush, tropical wonderland in central Florida, is one of the state's most popular tourist attractions. The "Miracle Strip" along the panhandle (right) contains the longest stretches of open, natural beach in Florida.

East of Tampa in the lake country of Winter Haven is Cypress Gardens. Waterskiing championships are held here each June. During the rest of the year, visitors marvel at waterskiing demonstrations and richly landscaped gardens.

A short distance north of Tampa, on coast-hugging U.S. 19, is Tarpon Springs, a quaint, predominantly Greek village that is one of the world's largest sponge markets. The town abounds in sponge-fishing traditions and lore. At Weeki Wachee Spring, glass-bottomed boats take visitors along shaded riverbanks. From a glassed-in auditorium built below the surface of the crystal-clear spring, spectators can watch "mermaids" perform underwater ballet. Weeki Wachee also presents a birds-of-prey show featuring hawks, owls, and a golden eagle. Homosassa Springs exhibits waterfowl and an underwater view of great schools of fish coursing through the spring.

At Crystal River, the main highway swings slightly inland to go around the Big Bend below the panhandle. Here, an interesting detour can be taken to the fishing village of Cedar Key. An 1896 hurricane destroyed the town's once-thriving pencil industry.

Now Cedar Key is a quiet, comfortable town with attractive shops and restaurants. A favorite local dish is smoked mullet and swamp-cabbage salad. Nearby are Chiefland and Manatee Springs State Park, great for a summer swim or a canoe trip down a clear river.

Along the panhandle coast, U.S. Route 98, known as the Miracle Strip Parkway, travels through historic St. Marks and the fishing town of Apalachicola. It continues west to Port St. Joe, a jumping-off place to wilderness beaches and some fine saltwater fishing. Farther up the coast is Panama City, a resort that abounds with amusement parks, golf courses, splendid beaches, and superb fishing. It is especially popular with summer vacationers from nearby southern states. Northwest of Panama City, U.S. 98 parallels the Gulf and the "Miracle Strip," a stretch of dazzling, white-sand beaches, for another 100 miles (161 kilometers) to Pensacola, where our journey began.

Contrary to the lyrics of the state song, Florida is no longer "far, far away" or "way down upon the Suwanee River." It is served by about thirty-three commercial airlines, modern interstate highways, cruise ships, and railroads. Its reputation as an all-season vacationland continues to grow, and its resident population is rising like a fast tide.

More people mean more pressure on Florida's natural and human resources. Coping with the ever-greater demands on its finances, law enforcement agencies, highways, schools, and natural resources while still maintaining a high-quality environment is both a problem and an objective. Florida's greatest challenge as it looks toward the twenty-first century will be how to protect its many delights for the growing population that wishes to enjoy them.

FACTS AT A GLANCE

GENERAL INFORMATION

Statehood: March 3, 1845, twenty-seventh state

Origin of Name: Spanish explorer Juan Ponce de León named the land *Florida* in April 1513. He arrived in Florida during the Spanish "Feast of Flowers," *Pascua Florida* (Easter). Some accounts suggest that he named Florida for the abundance of flowers he saw there.

State Capital: Tallahassee, selected as capital in 1824

State Nickname: "Sunshine State"; also called "Peninsula State"

State Flag: The current state flag was adopted in 1899. The Constitutional Convention of 1868 called for a state flag to have "the Great Seal of the State impressed upon a white ground of six feet six inches wide and six feet deep." The seal has, in the words of the 1868 legislature, "in the center thereof a view of the sun's rays over a high land in the distance, a cocoa tree, a steamboat on water, and an Indian female scattering flowers in the foreground encircled by the words, 'Great Seal of Florida: In God We Trust.' " In 1970 the legislature changed the wording in the official description from "cocoa tree" to "sabal palmetto palm," the state tree since 1953. The Indian woman stands for the importance of Indians in Florida's history. The sun symbolizes splendor and glory; the boat, commerce and growth; the palm tree, victory, honor, and justice; and the flowers, hope and joy. The official state flag of 1868 lacked color, so in 1899 the legislature moved to add diagonal red bars, which stand for the bars of the Confederate flag.

State Motto: "In God We Trust"

State Bird: Mockingbird

State Animal: Florida panther

State Mammal: Manatee in fresh water; dolphin in salt water

State Fish: Largemouth bass in fresh water; Atlantic sailfish in salt water

State Flower: Orange blossom

State Tree: Sabal palm (cabbage palm)

State Gem: Moonstone

State Shell: Florida horse conch

State Beverage: Orange juice

State Insect: Praying mantis

State Stone: Agatized coral

State Song: "Old Folks at Home," music and lyrics by Stephen Collins Foster; adopted as the official state song in 1935:

> Way down upon the Swanee River,
>   Far, far away,
> There's where my heart is turning ever,
>   There's where the old folks stay.
> All up and down the whole creation
>   Sadly I roam,
> Still longing for the old plantation,
>   And for the old folks at home.
>
> (CHORUS)
> All the world is sad and dreary,
>   Everywhere I roam;
> Oh brothers, how my heart grows weary,
> Far from the old folks at home!
>
> All round the little farm I wandered,
>   When I was young,
> Then many happy days I squandered,
>   Many the songs I sung.
> When I was playing with my brother,
>   Happy was I;
> Oh take me to my kind old mother!
>   There let me live and die.
>
> One little hut among the bushes,
>   One that I love,
> Still sadly to my memory rushes,
>   No matter where I rove.
> When will I see the bees a-humming
>   All 'round the comb?
> When will I hear the banjo strumming,
>   Down in my good old home?

POPULATION

Population: 9,746,421 (1980 census) fifth among the states (1987 estimate)

Population Density: 192 people per sq. mi. (74 people per km^2)

Population Distribution: 84.3 percent of the people live in urban areas.

Jacksonville	540,920
Miami	346,865
Tampa	271,523
St. Petersburg	238,647
Fort Lauderdale	153,279
Hialeah	145,254
Orlando	128,291
Hollywood	121,323
Miami Beach	96,298
Clearwater	85,528

(Population figures according to 1980 census)

Population Growth: Since the first territorial census in 1830, Florida's population has grown steadily and often dramatically. From 1970 to 1980, the state population increased 43.4 percent, the third-largest percentage of growth in the nation, while the nation grew at a rate of 11.45 percent. The list below shows population growth in Florida since 1830 according to United States census figures:

Year	·Population
1830	34,730
1850	87,445
1870	187,748
1890	391,422
1910	752,619
1930	1,468,211
1940	1,897,414
1950	2,771,305
1960	4,951,560
1970	6,791,418
1980	9,739,992

GEOGRAPHY

Borders: States that border Florida are Alabama on the north and west and Georgia on the north. On the east, Florida is bordered by the Atlantic Ocean. The Gulf of Mexico creates its southern and most of its western border.

Highest Point: Walton County, 345 ft. (105 m)

Sunset over Upper Myakka Lake in Myakka River State Park near Sarasota

Lowest Point: Sea level

Greatest Distances: North to south—447 mi. (719 km)
East to west—361 mi. (581 km)

Area: 54,090 sq. mi. (140,092 km²)

Rank in Area Among the States: Twenty-sixth

Rivers: Florida's Department of Natural Resources has catalogued 1,711 rivers, streams, and creeks. Thirty-four are "major" rivers, ranging from the 10-mi. (16-km) Wakulla River to the 275-mi. (442-km) St. Johns. The St. Johns, which flows northward from Melbourne into the Atlantic Ocean, is the most important river near Florida's east coast. The Perdido River in northwestern Florida, which marks part of the Florida-Alabama state line, flows into the Gulf of Mexico. During Spanish rule, the Apalachicola and its tributaries were Florida's most important rivers because they offered inland water routes to and from Georgia and Alabama. Today, the Apalachicola remains northwestern Florida's most important river. The famous Suwannee River, subject of the Florida state song, empties into the Gulf of Mexico after flowing southwestward through northern Florida. The St. Marys in northeastern Florida forms part of the Georgia-Florida boundary and empties into the Atlantic Ocean. Other major rivers are the Aucilla, Blackwater, Chipola, Choctawhatchee, Escambia, Hillsborough, Kissimmee, and Ochlockonee.

Lakes: Florida has about thirty thousand natural lakes, most of them in the central part of the state. Lake Okeechobee, which covers 448,000 acres (181,305 hectares), is the largest lake in Florida. It is also the third-largest freshwater lake lying wholly within the United States, and the second-largest entirely within one state. The largest artificial reservoir in the state is the Central and Southern Florida Flood Control District's Conservation Area No. 1 in the Everglades. It has a surface area of 216 sq. mi. (559 km²). Major natural lakes include Apopka, Crescent, George, Harris, Kissimmee, Orange, and Tohopekaliga.

One can see all the way to the bottom of crystal-clear Ichetucknee Springs.

Springs: Florida has seventeen of the country's seventy-five artesian springs. Silver Springs in Florida's central region is the state's largest spring. Wakulla Springs in the northern part of the state is one of the deepest springs in the country, with a depth of 185 ft. (56 m).

Topography: The state is usually divided into six natural regions. The Coastal Lowlands include the entire coast and the Florida Keys. The uniformly flat Coastal Lowlands include a variety of habitats—forest, open prairie, swamp, and dune— and reach inland as far as 60 mi. (97 km).

The Western Highlands in the northwestern panhandle are relatively hilly with several narrow, steep-walled valleys. The land is generally pine-covered and only sparsely settled.

The Marianna Lowlands are west of the Apalachicola River in Washington, Holmes, and Jackson counties. Surrounded by the Western Highlands, the hills here are low and rolling.

Rolling hills and gentle slopes characterize the Tallahassee Hills region, which reaches north of Tallahassee to the Georgia border and includes part of the northeast panhandle.

The Central Highlands occupy much of the central peninsula from the Georgia border and Okefenokee Swamp south to a point just north of Lake Okeechobee. Much of the region, particularly south of Ocala, consists of rolling hills and thousands of lakes.

The Everglades, the Big Cypress Swamp, and the Okefenokee Swamp form the sixth type of natural region in Florida. The Big Cypress Swamp and the Everglades together virtually cover the southern tip of Florida, most of the region south of Lake Okeechobee, and a region adjacent to the eastern shore of the lake. The Everglades is a broad, 1,200-sq.-mi. (3,108-km²) depression. Okefenokee is a 660-sq.-mi. (1,709-km²) wetland that straddles the Georgia-Florida border. Just 66 sq. mi. (171 km²) of Okefenokee extends into Florida.

Climate: Florida summers are long, relatively humid, and warm. Winters are mild, though often interrupted by cool or cold air from the north. Coastal areas are slightly warmer in winter and cooler in summer than inland sites at the same latitude. The southeast coast and the Florida Keys enjoy the warmest winters because of the warming influence of the Gulf Stream current and prevailing southern winds. The average January temperature is 54° F. (12° C) in northern Florida (Tallahassee) and 67° F. (19° C) in southern Florida (Miami). Summer temperatures in both Tallahassee and Miami average 82° F. (28° C) in July.

Rainfall in Florida ranges from an average of 50 inches (128 cm) to 65 in. (166 cm) per year. The highest rainfall occurs in the extreme northwest and at the southern tip of the peninsula. The Keys, which are south of the peninsula, receive an annual rainfall of just 40 in. (102 cm). Florida tends to have a summer "rainy season" followed by relatively dry winters. Excessive rainfall, tempered by periodic drought, is part of the natural cycle in Florida. Violent storms are common. Florida is one of the ten most-tornado-prone states. Hurricanes, though relatively rare, threaten between June and October. Hurricanes are an important source of water in south Florida.

Although snowfall is extremely rare in Florida, no place on the Florida mainland is entirely safe from the possibility of frost. Cold waves, however, seldom last more than a day or two and rarely penetrate into southern Florida.

The highest recorded temperature in Florida was 109° F. (43° C) at Monticello on June 29, 1931. A record low -2° F. (-19° C) was reached at Tallahassee on February 13, 1899.

NATURE

Trees: Approximately 350 species, representing about half of all species known in the United States, grow in Florida. Native trees include slash pine, longleaf pine, bald cypress, southern red cedar, sabal palm, southern bayberry, water hickory, laurel oak, live oak, strangler fig, sweetbay, custard-apple, Bahama lysiloma, gumbo-limbo, red maple, red mangrove, black tupelo, and Florida fiddlewood.

Wild Plants: Approximately 3,500 species of wild plants grow in Florida. Among the notable flowering plants are lupines, sunflowers, water lilies, wood lilies, spider lilies, coreopsis, irises, mallows, marsh pinks, azaleas, camellias, oleanders,

The sandhill crane is one of the many species of colorful birds that can be seen in Florida.

gardenias, hibiscus, bougainvillea, golden begonias, magnolias, dogwoods, red buds, over a hundred species of wild orchids, seven types of pitcher plants, and several species of cacti and bromeliads.

Animals: Approximately 90 species of mammals live in Florida, including the Florida panther, Key deer, mangrove fox squirrel, gray fox, opossum, striped skunk, spotted skunk, raccoon, black bear, river otter, marsh rabbit, manatee, and bottle-nosed dolphin. Some 150 species of reptiles and amphibians live in Florida, including the American alligator, American crocodile, pine barrens treefrog, Florida bog frog, green sea turtle, loggerhead sea turtle, indigo snake, gopher tortoise, eastern coral snake, and Florida box turtle.

Birds: More than 400 species of birds have been found in Florida, including the robin, red-winged blackbird, redheaded woodpecker, bobwhite quail, wild turkey, ibis, great egret, great blue heron, bald eagle, osprey, pileated woodpecker, roseate spoonbill, wood stork, reddish egret, black-bellied tree duck, pelican, and anhinga. The mangrove cuckoo and white-crowned pigeon are among the birds whose entire United States range is limited to south Florida.

Fish: Approximately 200 species of freshwater fish live in Florida lakes and rivers. Some are actually saltwater species, such as striped bass and tarpon, that enter tidal streams. True freshwater fish in the state include spotted gar, chubs, white catfish, yellow catfish, killfish, Suwannee bass, Chipola bass, Florida largemouth bass, shellcracker, bluegill (bream), and crappie (speckled perch). About 1,200 species of marine fish live in Florida salt water, including pompano, bluefish, grouper, red snapper, menhaden, sailfish, mackerel, sea trout, and marlin.

GOVERNMENT

Florida's government consists of legislative, executive, and judicial branches. The state legislature consists of a 40-member state senate and a 120-member house of representatives. Senators are elected to four-year terms, and house members serve two-year terms. The state legislature passes laws only after the senate and house agree on a measure. Amendments to Florida's constitution may be proposed by the legislature, but must be approved by the state's voters.

The executive branch enforces the laws and runs the government. Florida's executive branch is unique among the states in that the governor and his cabinet share executive responsibility. The cabinet is made up of six elected officials: attorney general, commissioner of agriculture, comptroller, secretary of state, commissioner of education, and treasurer.

The judicial branch determines the constitutionality of laws, policies, and programs, and settles any conflicts arising from interpretation and application of the laws. The judicial branch consists of a state supreme court, five district courts of appeal, twenty circuit courts, and sixty-one county courts, each with one or more judges. The Florida Supreme Court is the state's highest tribunal. It has seven justices appointed by the governor to serve six-year terms. Judges who wish to remain on the court can place their names on the ballot for a retention vote at a general election. The chief justice of the supreme court is chosen by other justices of the court. Chief justices traditionally serve two years.

Number of Counties: 67

U.S. Representatives: 19

Electoral Votes: 21

Voting Qualifications: Eighteen years of age, United States citizen, resident of state for a minimum of one year, resident of the same Florida county for at least six months

EDUCATION

Formal, statewide education began with the ratification of the state constitution of 1868. In the late 1980s, Florida spent an average of $3,731 on each public school student. There were 823,000 grade school students and 736,000 secondary students in 2,200 public schools. Another 208,000 students (kindergarten through grade twelve) attended private schools.

Florida has more than thirty fully accredited private and public universities and colleges. The largest is the University of Florida at Gainesville, with an enrollment exceeding thirty-six thousand. The University of Florida at Gainesville and Florida State University at Tallahassee can trace their roots to 1823, when Congress reserved "seminary lands" for two institutions of higher learning in the Florida territory. Other state-operated institutions include Florida A & M in Tallahassee, Florida Atlantic in Boca Raton, Florida International in North Miami, the University of Central Florida in Orlando, the University of North Florida in

Citrus fruit is Florida's most important agricultural product.

Jacksonville, the University of South Florida in Tampa, and the University of West Florida in Pensacola. Among the best-known private colleges and universities are the University of Miami in Coral Gables, Florida Southern in Lakeland, Rollins College in Winter Park, Stetson University in DeLand, the University of Tampa, and Jacksonville University. Florida has twenty-eight community colleges.

ECONOMY AND INDUSTRY

Principal Products

Agriculture: Citrus fruit (oranges, grapefruit, limes, tangerines, tangelos), watermelon, cotton, strawberries, bananas, cantaloupes, pineapples, papayas, mangoes, avocados, cucumbers, peas, celery, tomatoes, peppers, sugarcane, beef cattle, hogs, peanuts, pecans, milk, corn, hay, oats, tobacco, wheat

Manufacturing: Food products, electric and electronic equipment, transportation equipment, paper, tung oil, cigars, storage batteries, chemicals

Natural Resources: Favorable climate, phosphate, fertile soil, oil, forests, shellfish, marine fish, titanium, limestone, fuller's earth, mineral sands, brick clay, kaolin (a pottery clay), peat

Business and Industry: Tourism, which is a year-round business in Florida, is the largest income-producing activity in the state. Every year, about 40 million tourists visit the state, spending a total of about $22 billion. Service industries, many of which are associated with tourism, account for almost 80 percent of Florida's gross state product (the total value of goods and services produced annually). Manufacturing is the next-most-important economic activity. Processed foods, particularly citrus-fruit products, lead the list of manufactured products, bringing in about $3 billion per year. Every year, citrus-processing plants produce about 170 million gal. (644 million l) of frozen orange juice, as well as canned fruit and other citrus by-products. Frozen vegetables and canned seafood are other important processed foods. Florida is a major commercial-fishing state. Florida's annual catch, which totals about 194 million lbs. (88 million kg) of fish, brings in about $170 million.

117

Cruise ships docked at the Port of Miami

Communication: Florida has about 250 newspapers. About 60 of these are published daily. Jacksonville's *Florida Times-Union*, established in 1864, is Florida's oldest newspaper. Other important daily newspapers are the *Fort Lauderdale News, Miami Herald, Miami News, Pensacola Journal, St. Petersburg Times, Orlando Sentinel-Star, Tampa Tribune,* and *Sarasota Tribune.* In 1980 Miami had eleven Spanish-language newspapers. The largest is *El Diario/La Prensa.* The *Miami Herald* prints a Spanish-language edition. The state has 350 radio stations and 60 television stations. WFAW, later WQAM in Miami, began broadcasting on a 50-watt transmitter in 1920. Miami's WTVJ-TV began television broadcasting in 1949.

Transportation: With its proximity to Latin America and the West Indies and its heavy tourist traffic, Florida is a strategic and busy transportation center. It is the third-busiest state in volume of aircraft activity. The state has 502 licensed airports, of which 140 are public and 22 are military. Some 15 million people fly into Florida each year. Sixteen major public airports and about 33 commercial airlines serve Florida.

Florida has 6,556 mi. (10,549 km) of railway, with fifteen railroad companies offering freight service throughout much of the state. Passenger service reaches about twenty Florida cities. The state has 97,000 miles (156,073 km) of roads, two-thirds of them surfaced.

In 1980, Florida's eight major seaports exported goods valued at over $6 billion and imported goods worth more than $5 billion. The busiest Florida seaports are at Miami, Tampa, Jacksonville, Port Canaveral, Palm Beach, Port Everglades (Fort Lauderdale), Pensacola, and Panama City. Among Florida's navigable inland waterways, only the St. Johns River and Okeechobee Waterway have much freight traffic. Pleasure craft can cross the state via the St. Lucie Canal, Lake Okeechobee, and the Caloosahatchee River, which flows into the Gulf of Mexico. Boaters traveling from north to south can navigate the Atlantic Intracoastal Waterway along Florida's east coast or the Gulf Intracoastal Waterway on the west coast.

SOCIAL AND CULTURAL LIFE

Museums: Florida has about thirty major art museums. Situated on beautifully landscaped grounds, the John and Mable Ringling Museum of Art in Sarasota houses one of the world's finest collections of Baroque art. It is especially noted for having one of the country's best collections of paintings by Peter Paul Rubens. Other fine art museums are the Lowe Art Museum at the University of Miami, the Cummer Gallery of Art in Jacksonville, the Center for the Fine Arts in Miami, the Loch Haven Art Center in Orlando, the Florida State University Fine Arts Gallery in Tallahassee, the Society of the Four Arts in Palm Beach, Viscaya Museum of Art and Gardens near Miami, the Museum of Fine Arts in St. Petersburg, and the Norton Gallery and School of Art in West Palm Beach. The Florida State Museum in Gainesville is the state's largest historical, natural history, and science museum. Specialized museums include the Beal Maltbie Shell Museum in Winter Park, the Air Force Armament Museum in Eglin Field near Fort Walton Beach, the Edison Museum in Fort Myers, the Museum of the Circus in Sarasota, and the Naval Aviation Museum in Pensacola.

Libraries: Florida has approximately 345 public libraries, of which 215 are county or regional branches. The Florida Department of State supervises the State Library of Florida in Tallahassee. The P.K. Yonge Library of Florida History contains the best collection of books about Florida, and is the largest research library in the state. It is housed at the University of Florida in Gainesville.

Performing Arts: Florida's most renowned theater is the Asolo State Theater in Sarasota, which offers a professional training program in association with Florida State University. Other theaters of note in Florida are the Coconut Grove Playhouse in Miami and the Hippodrome Street Theater in Gainesville. Tampa is proud of its Performing Arts Center, which opened in 1987.

Major symphonies include the Florida Orchestra of St. Petersburg, Tampa, and Clearwater; the Florida Symphony Orchestra of Orlando; the Jacksonville Symphony Orchestra; and the Philharmonic Orchestra of Florida at Fort Lauderdale. The Greater Miami Opera is one of the nation's most respected companies. The Gainesville Civic Ballet, the Florida Ballet of Jacksonville, and the Southern Ballet Theater of Winter Park perform for dance enthusiasts.

Sports and Recreation: Eighteen major-league baseball teams hold spring training in Florida from about March 1 through early April. Thousands of Florida spectators can watch them in the Florida Grapefruit-League games. Florida has two National Football League teams, the Miami Dolphins and the Tampa Bay Buccaneers. The Tampa Bay Rowdies and the Fort Lauderdale Strikers are Florida's professional soccer teams. Other popular spectator sports include professional horse racing, greyhound racing, and jai alai.

Florida's beaches, warm climate, and sunny days provide an ideal environment for outdoor recreation. Floridians participate in tennis, golf, softball, basketball, water sports, shell collecting, shuffleboard, fossil collecting, spelunking (cave exploration), fishing, hunting, hiking, and bird-watching.

Floridians and tourists alike enjoy taking advantage of the state's ninety-two state parks and historic memorials. Some of the more interesting state parks include Myakka River State Park near Sarasota , an exceptional wildlife preserve that includes a 7,500-acre (3,035-hectare) wilderness area for hikers only; Highlands Hammock State Park near Sebring, which includes a cypress swamp accessible by boardwalk and offers wildlife tours taken on a "trackless train"; John Pennekamp Coral Reef State Park at Key Largo, which was the nation's first underwater preserve and features part of the only living coral reef in North America; Torreya State Park between Bristol and Greensboro in the panhandle, which has remnant populations of northern plants and animals left by retreating glaciers some twelve thousand years ago; Manatee Springs State Park near Chiefland, which surrounds one of the most beautiful springs in the country; Florida Caverns State Park in Marianna, which includes a network of dramatic limestone caverns and caves; and Lake Kissimmee State Park near Lake Wales, which provides a "living history" demonstration of nineteenth-century cowboy life on the Kissimmee prairies. Bahia Honda State Recreation Area on Bahia Honda Key contains the most beautiful beaches in the Keys. Sebastian Inlet State Recreation Area, a beautiful park situated on a barrier island, is the most popular state park in Florida and provides the finest surfing in the state. Located at the site of an old Spanish salvage camp, the park includes the McLarty State Museum, which has the state's finest collection of recovered Spanish gold.

Florida has four state forests: Blackwater River, Withlacoochee, Cary, and Pine Log. The state also has three national forests: Apalachicola National Forest in northwestern Florida, Ocala National Forest in central Florida, and Osceola National Forest near Lake City.

Everglades National Park, which covers almost all of the southern tip of the state, is the largest subtropical wilderness in North America. This unique land of sawgrass, water, and tree islands, sometimes referred to as a "river of grass," is one of the country's most popular tourist attractions. Boardwalks, trails, canoe routes, and airboat tours take visitors deep into this remarkable wetland. Just north of the Everglades, Big Cypress National Preserve covers 570,000 acres (230,679 hectares) of The Big Cypress Swamp.

Florida has two national seashores: Canaveral National Seashore, which contains the largest strip of undeveloped wilderness beach in Florida; and Gulf Islands National Seashore, a 150-mi. (241-km) stretch of offshore islands and keys that runs from Destin in the panhandle to Gulfport, Mississippi.

Historic Sites and Landmarks:

Bulow Plantation Ruins State Historic Site, near Bunnell Beach, was the site of a plantation that was destroyed in the Second Seminole War. Visitors can see the crumbling foundation of the mansion, the remains of an old coquina sugar mill, and some well-preserved wells.

Castillo de San Marcos National Monument in St. Augustine is a massive, imposing coquina fort built by the Spanish between 1672 and 1695.

Crystal River State Archaeological Site, northwest of Crystal River, is the site of a ceremonial center that was occupied by Indians from about 200 B.C. to A.D. 1400. A museum at the site permits visitors to view burial, ceremonial, and refuse mounds through plate-glass windows.

Dade Battlefield State Historic Site in Bushnell is the site of the start of the Second Seminole War. Here, in 1835, the Seminole attacked Major Francis Dade and his troops. A nature trail follows Dade's route through the pines.

De Soto National Memorial, at the mouth of the Manatee River, is believed to be the site of Hernando De Soto's landing in 1539.

Fort Caroline Memorial, east of Jacksonville, is a reconstruction of the sixteenth-century French fort that was destroyed by the Spanish in 1565.

Fort Gadsden State Historic Site, in Apalachicola National Forest near Sumatra, was the site of an abandoned British fort that was held by a group of Choctaw Indians and runaway slaves during the War of 1812. American forces destroyed the fort in 1816, killing nearly three hundred people. General Andrew Jackson had the fort rebuilt when he invaded Spanish Florida in 1818, and this garrison was maintained until Florida was ceded to the United States.

Fort Jefferson National Monument, on Garden Key in the Dry Tortugas, is the largest brick fort in the Western Hemisphere. Construction of the fort began in 1846 and continued for thirty years. After the Civil War, the fort was used as a prison.

Fort Matanzas, south of St. Augustine on Rattlesnake Island, was built by the Spanish in the 1740s. The area also marks the spot of the 1565 massacre of some three hundred French Huguenots by Spanish colonists.

Gamble Plantation State Historic Site, north of Bradenton, is a mansion that has been restored to look as it did in the 1840s when it was part of a huge sugar plantation.

Kingsley Plantation State Historic Site, on Fort George Island, is a restored nineteenth-century home that has been furnished with antiques and has exhibits about the history of the area. Built in 1813 by rugged individualist Zephaniah Kingsley, it is believed to be the oldest remaining plantation house in Florida.

Koreshan State Historic Site, south of Fort Myers in Estero, is the site of a nineteenth-century Utopian community established by members of the Koreshan Unity, led by religious visionary Cyrus Reed Teed. Arriving from Chicago in 1894, Teed and his followers beautifully transformed the wild pineland by building homes, roads, footpaths, and trails.

Olustee Battlefield State Historic Site, near Olustee, has an annual reenactment of the battle fought here in 1864. The battlefield lies at the end of a well-marked trail through the pine woods.

Pensacola Historic District, a national historic landmark, exhibits restored homes, the oldest church in Florida (Christ Church, built in 1832), and numerous museums, art galleries, and antique shops.

Marjorie Kinnan Rawlings State Historic Site, near Gainesville, is a nineteenth-century "Cracker" house with rambling porches and wooden siding. For thirteen years it was the home of Rawlings, author of *Cross Creek* and *The Yearling*.

San Agustin Antiguo (Old St. Augustine) is a section of St. Augustine that has been restored to look like an eighteenth-century Spanish colonial village.

San Marcos de Apalache State Historic Site, near St. Marks, is located at the junction of the St. Marks and Wakulla rivers. A nature trail and boardwalk lead to the fort site, where a considerable amount of Florida history was made as Spanish, Indian, British, and American forces jockeyed for possession of what was once strategic swampland.

Yulee Sugar Mill State Historic Site, near Homosassa Springs, preserves the ruins of an 1851 sugar mill that stood on a 5,100-acre (2,064-hectare) sugar plantation owned by Florida's first United States senator, David Levy Yulee. Some of the mill's original machinery is on display.

Other Interesting Places to Visit:

Bok Tower Gardens, at Lake Wales, is a beautifully landscaped garden that was donated to the state by Edward Bok in 1929. A carillon of fifty-three bronze bells housed in the 205-ft. (62-m) Bok Tower chimes out a concert every day at 3 P.M.

Corkscrew Swamp Sanctuary, near Naples, a relic of the magnificent bald cypress forests that were virtually logged out in Florida by the mid-1950s, features the largest remaining stand of virgin bald cypress in the country. A boardwalk takes visitors through a forested wetland of huge, seven-hundred-year-old cypress trees. Thousands of rare birds can be spotted at the sanctuary.

Cypress Gardens, near Winter Haven, is a lush, tropical wonderland of moss-draped cypresses, exotic plants, lagoons, grottoes, and winding walkways. Famous for its water-ski shows and electric-boat rides, it is one of Florida's oldest and most enduring tourist attractions.

Dark Continent/Busch Gardens in Tampa is an African theme park that features thrill rides, exotic wildlife, and a monorail ride through a recreation of an African plain.

Jay Norwood "Ding" Darling National Wildlife Refuge, on Sanibel Island, is one of the finest areas in Florida for wildlife observation. A five-mi. (eight-km) unpaved road travels through a mangrove swamp and provides a unique look at alligators, ospreys, roseate spoonbills, and dozens of other species of animals.

Thomas A. Edison Winter Home and Gardens in Fort Myers preserves Thomas Edison's winter residence, guest house, laboratory, and gardens. A museum contains hundreds of Edison inventions, including movie cameras, early light bulbs, and 170 gramophones.

Killer whales perform regularly at Sea World, the world's largest marine park.

Kennedy Space Center at Cape Canaveral has exhibits that dramatize the history of American space exploration. Tour buses take visitors to the huge Vehicle Assembly Building, Mission Control, the Astronaut Training Facility, and launch pads.

Lion Country Safari near West Palm Beach is a drive-through wildlife preserve where more than a thousand animals, including lions, giraffes, zebras, antelopes, elephants, and ostriches, roam free.

Maclay State Ornamental Gardens, in Tallahassee, is one of the finest ornamental gardens in the Southeast. The U.S. champion flowering dogwood grows here, along with thousands of azaleas, camellias, and ornamentals.

Marineland, near St. Augustine, established in 1938, is the world's oldest marine park. It features the Aquarius Theater, where porpoises perform six times a day; an electric eel demonstration; and oceanariums filled with more than a hundred kinds of marine animals.

Merritt Island National Wildlife Refuge, east of Titusville, contains 139,000 acres (56,253 hectares) of forest, lake, and marsh, and is the natural habitat of more than 250 species of birds. The refuge is also home to more endangered and threatened wildlife species than any United States refuge outside of Hawaii. Among its rare residents are green sea turtles, wood storks, and bald eagles.

Metrozoo in Miami is a cageless zoo that houses one of the largest animal collections in the country.

St. Marks National Wildlife Refuge, south of Tallahassee, is a wet wilderness that spreads over 64,000 acres (25,901 hectares). A road penetrating a small section of the refuge enables visitors to see alligators and a variety of water birds.

Sea World, near Orlando, is the largest marine park in the world. It features performances by superbly trained killer whales, dolphins, and seals, as well as marine exhibits and a water-ski show.

Silver Springs, near Ocala, has a deep, crystal-clear spring, beautiful landscaped gardens, and a reptile show.

Walt Disney World Vacation Kingdom in Lake Buena Vista is an elaborate entertainment and resort complex that claims to be the world's most popular tourist attraction. Disney World's original theme park, the Magic Kingdom, is divided into six different "lands": Main Street U.S.A., Adventureland, Frontierland, Liberty Square, Fantasyland, and Tomorrowland. EPCOT Center (Experimental Prototype Community of Tomorrow), which opened in 1982, has two dimensions: Future World, which provides a look at the world of tomorrow; and World Showcase, which presents the customs and lifestyles of nations around the world.

IMPORTANT DATES

8000 B.C.-A.D.1500 — Semipermanent and permanent Indian settlements established

1513 — Juan Ponce de León lands in Florida and claims it for Spain

1528 — Pánfilo de Narváez leads an expedition to Florida's southwestern coast

1539 — Hernando De Soto lands in the Tampa Bay area

1564 — René de Goulaine de Laudonnière and some three hundred French Huguenots build Fort Caroline on the St. Johns River

1565 — Admiral Pedro Menéndez de Avilés captures Fort Caroline, massacres most of its French population, and establishes St. Augustine, the first permanent European settlement in the United States

1586 — Sir Francis Drake of England burns and loots St. Augustine

1698 — The Spanish complete Castillo de San Marcos at St. Augustine; a permanent Spanish settlement in Pensacola is established

1702-03 — The British attack St. Augustine and destroy Spanish missions in North Florida

1719 — The French capture Pensacola

1723 — The French return Pensacola to Spain

1740 — British General James Oglethorpe of Georgia attacks St. Augustine

1750 — Creek Indians accompanied by a few runaway slaves migrate to Florida, where they eventually become known as Seminole

1763—Spain cedes Florida to England in exchange for Havana, Cuba

1777—The British attack Savannah, Georgia, from St. Augustine during the
     American Revolution

1781—The Spanish capture Pensacola; the British surrender West Florida to Spain

1783—Spain regains the rest of Florida from England in exchange for the Bahamas;
     Florida's first newspaper, the *East Florida Gazette*, is published in St. Augustine

1812—Encouraged by the American government, settlers in East Florida rebel
     against Spanish authority; when the rebellion falters, the government withdraws
     its support

1814—American General Andrew Jackson captures, then abandons, Pensacola

1817-18—First Seminole War; Jackson again captures Pensacola

1819—Spain agrees to cede East and West Florida to the United States

1821—Treaty deeding Florida to the United States is ratified

1822—The United States unifies East and West Florida; William P. DuVal becomes
     first territorial governor of united Florida

1824—Tallahassee selected as Florida's territorial capital

1835—Dade Massacre touches off the Second Seminole War

1836—Florida's first railroads begin operating

1837—Seminole leader Osceola is betrayed and captured while meeting with
     United States soldiers under a flag of truce

1839—State constitution is drawn up

1842—Second Seminole War ends with the near-destruction of the Seminole
     people; only a few hundred Seminole remain in Florida

1845—Florida admitted into the Union as a slaveholding state; William D. Moseley
     becomes first state governor

1855—Florida passes first Internal Improvement Act to build roads and canals

1855-58—Third Seminole War

1860—First cross-state railroad completed

1861—Florida secedes from the Union and joins the Confederacy; Civil War begins

1864—Battle of Olustee results in Confederate victory and the protection of interior supply lines from Florida to Georgia

1865—Civil War ends; slavery abolished; Florida placed under United States military rule

1868—New state constitution drafted; voting rights given to blacks; free school system established

1877—Reconstruction ends as the last federal troops leave Florida

1881—Hamilton Disston of Philadelphia buys 4 million acres (1.6 million hectares) of land in central Florida, paving the way for development of the peninsula

1883—Henry Flagler begins construction of Florida's East Coast Railway

1889—State medical board created in response to several yellow-fever epidemics; poll tax introduced to decrease number of black voters

1894-95—Severe frosts in North Florida force citrus growers to move southward

1912—Last leg of the East Coast Railway, the 128-mile (206-km) Overseas Railway from Homestead to Key West, is completed

1914—First regularly scheduled commercial air travel between United States cities established between St. Petersburg and Tampa

1924—Florida land boom begins

1926—Land boom collapses; a hurricane kills hundreds of people in Dade County

1928—South Florida is hit by another hurricane; at least eighteen hundred are killed in the Okeechobee area

1933—Chicago Mayor Anton Cermak is fatally wounded in Miami during assassination attempt on President-elect Franklin D. Roosevelt

1935—Labor Day hurricane kills four hundred in Florida Keys and destroys Overseas Railway

1938—Overseas Highway is opened

1942—Florida resorts are converted into training camps for World War II soldiers; Four German agents on a sabotage mission land at Ponte Vedra

1950—Cape Canaveral opens as a space-research and rocket-testing center

1954—Sunshine Skyway across Lower Tampa Bay completed; U.S. Supreme Court rules that schools and other public facilities must be racially integrated

1958 — Explorer I, the first American satellite, is launched into orbit from Cape Canaveral

1960-61 — Thousands of Cuban refugees arrive in southeast Florida

1962 — Astronaut John H. Glenn, Jr. becomes the first American to orbit the earth after being launched from Cape Canaveral

1969 — Apollo 11, launched from Cape Canaveral, lands the first men on the moon; Florida schools integrated

1971 — Walt Disney World theme park opens in Lake Buena Vista near Orlando; a state corporate-profits tax, Florida's first income tax, is adopted

1980 — Mariel Boatlift brings 120,000 Cuban refugees to Florida; a freighter strikes Sunshine Skyway, killing thirty-five people and destroying the southbound span; race riots in Miami are touched off by the acquittal of four policemen accused of beating to death a black businessman and eighteen people are killed in the disorder

1986 — Space shuttle Challenger explodes seventy-three seconds after launch from Cape Canaveral, killing all seven aboard

IMPORTANT PEOPLE

Reubin Askew (1928-   ), politician; governor of Florida (1971-79); first Florida governor to be elected to a second successive term; United States trade representative under President Jimmy Carter

William Bartram (1739-1823), naturalist, adventurer; traveled extensively in Florida and the Southeast; explored St. Johns River country in 1765-66; in 1791 published *The Travels of William Bartram*

Judah Philip Benjamin (1811-1894), Confederate secretary of state; hid at Gamble Plantation in Bradenton while trying to escape to England at the close of the Civil War

Mary McLeod Bethune (1875-1955), educator; in 1904 established Daytona Normal and Industrial Institute for girls, which in 1923 merged with the all-male Cookman Institute to become Bethune-Cookman College; president of college (1923-42, 1946-47); director of Division of Negro Affairs of the National Youth Administration (1936-44); founded National Council of Negro Women; special advisor to President Franklin D. Roosevelt on problems of minorities

JUDAH P. BENJAMIN

MARY M. BETHUNE

127

ARCHIE F. CARR

MARJORY S. DOUGLAS

CHRIS EVERT-LLOYD

CARL FISHER

Napoleon Broward (1857-1910), military leader and politician; in 1896 landed soldiers and supplies in Cuba during Cuban Civil War; governor of Florida (1905-09); as governor, implemented drainage of the Everglades and instituted consolidated state university system

James (Jimmy) Buffett (1947-   ), musician; composer and performer of such popular ballads about Florida as "Changes in Latitudes, Changes in Attitudes"

Archie F. Carr (1909-1987), biologist, educator, author; international authority on reptiles; books include *So Excellent a Fishe*, and *The Reptiles, Amphibians, and Freshwater Fishes of Florida*

Alvin Wentworth Chapman (1809-1899), physician and botanist; authority on Florida plant life and author of *Flora of the Southern United States*

Jacqueline Cochran (1912-1980), born in Pensacola; aviator; organized and directed the Women Air Force Service Pilots in World War II; first civilian woman to receive the Distinguished Service Medal

John S. Collins (1837-1928), horticulturist; initiated development of Miami Beach as a resort center after his plan to start a coconut plantation there failed

Francis Langhorne Dade (1793?-1835), military officer; ambush and massacre of Dade and his troops by Seminole was the event that touched off the Second Seminole War

Walter Elias (Walt) Disney (1901-1966), artist, film producer, entrepreneur; creator of famous animated characters Mickey Mouse and Donald Duck; produced the first full-length animated films; developed Disney Land theme park in Anaheim, California, and Walt Disney World theme park in Lake Buena Vista, Florida

Hamilton Disston (1844-1896), industrialist; in 1881 purchased 4 million acres (1.6 million hectares) of land in central Florida and paved the way for development of the area

Marjory Stoneman Douglas (1890-   ), historian, author; among her books on Florida is the classic *The Everglades: River of Grass*

Thomas Alva Edison (1847-1931), inventor; wintered in Fort Myers; perfected the incandescent lamp; was issued more than a thousand patents; among his most important inventions were a moving picture camera and the phonograph

Christine Marie (Chris) Evert-Lloyd (1953-   ), born in Fort Lauderdale; professional tennis champion; one of the top players in the world during the 1970s and 1980s

Carl Fisher (1874-1939), real estate developer; helped transform Miami Beach from a deserted mangrove swamp off the coast of Miami into a beautiful beach resort by clearing the area and adding sand dredged from the bottom of Biscayne Bay

Melvin (Mel) Fisher (1922-   ), professional treasure hunter; his salvage team located the gold-rich Spanish galleons *Atocha* and *Santa Margarita*, which sank in 1622 off the Florida Keys

MEL FISHER

Henry Morrison Flagler (1830-1913), industrialist; responsible for railroad and hotel development of Florida's east coast, especially Overseas Railway from Homestead to Key West, completed in 1912

Jackie Gleason (1916-1987), entertainer; broadcast his popular television shows *The Jackie Gleason Show* and *The Honeymooners* from Miami Beach

John Gorrie (1803-1855), physician and inventor; lived in Apalachicola most of his life; first in the United States to patent a mechanical refrigeration machine, which he invented for the purpose of cooling the sickrooms of fever patients

Robert (Bob) Graham (1936-   ), politician; governor of Florida (1979-87); member of United States Senate (1987-   )

Ernest Miller Hemingway (1899-1961), major American author; worked in Key West from 1928-40; while living there wrote such famous works as *A Farewell to Arms, For Whom the Bell Tolls,* and *To Have and Have Not,* which is set in the Keys

ERNEST HEMINGWAY

Zora Neale Hurston (1903-1960), born in Eatonville; folklorist and writer; became associated with the Harlem Renaissance; celebrated the culture of rural, southern blacks in such works as *Mules and Men,* a collection of folktales; also wrote novels, including the controversial *Their Eyes Were Watching God;* and an autobiography, *Dust Tracks on a Road*

Andrew Jackson (1767-1845), seventh president of the United States; military leader known as "Old Hickory"; conducted military campaigns in Florida prior to American possession of the territory; in 1814 captured Pensacola, a Spanish post that was being occupied by the British; invaded Florida again in 1818 during the First Seminole War, during which he defeated the Seminole and again captured Pensacola; his bold actions hastened United States acquisition of Florida; first United States commissioner and governor of East and West Florida (1822); president (1829-37)

ZORA NEALE HURSTON

Thomas Sidney Jessup (1788-1860), military leader; as commander of United States forces during the Second Seminole War, he betrayed a flag of truce to capture Seminole leader Osceola in 1837

James Weldon Johnson (1871-1938), poet, anthropologist; secretary of the National Association for the Advancement of Colored People; United States Consul in Venezuela and Nicaragua

MacKinlay Kantor (1904-1977), war correspondent, author; won Medal of Freedom for service in Korea; wrote fictional but carefully documented *Andersonville,* an account of the notorious Confederate prison that won the 1956 Pulitzer Prize in fiction

ANDREW JACKSON

CLAUDE KIRK

SIDNEY LANIER

PEDRO MENÉNDEZ

MARSHALL NIRENBERG

Edmund Kirby-Smith (1824-1893), born in St. Augustine; military officer; commanded Confederate forces west of the Mississippi; last Confederate commander to surrender at the end of the Civil War; mathematics instructor at West Point; president of the University of Nashville (1870-75)

Claude Kirk (1926-   ), politician; governor of Florida (1967-71); first Republican elected governor of Florida since 1877

René Goulaine de Laudonnière (1529?-1574), French Huguenot explorer and colonist; in 1564 founded Fort Caroline, a French colony near the mouth of the St. Johns River; escaped massacre of Huguenot settlers by the Spanish in 1565 and returned to France; wrote about his experiences in *L'Histoire notable de la Floride*

Sidney Lanier (1842-1881), poet and author; wrote early guide book to Florida, *Florida: its Scenery, Climate*, and *History*

Jacques de Morgues Le Moyne (?-1588), French artist and writer; accompanied René de Laudonnière on his 1564 expedition to Florida; was the first known professional European artist to visit the continental United States; wrote an account of the expedition that included drawings and descriptions of the Timucuan Indians he encountered; the work, later published in Europe, gave Europeans some of their earliest exposure to Native American life

Lue Gim Gong (1858-1925), horticulturist; developed late-ripening, frost-resistant orange

John Dann MacDonald (1916-1986), writer; lived in Sarasota; author of detective novels featuring the character Travis McGee, including *The Deep Blue Goodbye, The Dreadful Lemon Sky*, and *The Lonely Silver Rain*; other works include *The Last One Left, The Green Ripper*, and *Condominium*

Pedro Menéndez de Avilés (1519-1574), Spanish explorer; sent to Florida by King Philip II to explore, colonize, and defend the area; in 1565 founded St. Augustine, the first permanent European settlement in what would become the United States; massacred the French Huguenot colony at Fort Caroline

Addison Mizner (1872-1933), architect; designer of lavish, pseudo-Spanish hotels and houses in Boca Raton and Palm Beach, including the Everglades Club and the Boca Raton Club

Samuel Alexander Mudd (1833-1883), physician; was unjustly convicted of conspiracy for treating John Wilkes Booth's broken leg after Booth assassinated President Abraham Lincoln; while imprisoned at Fort Jefferson in the Dry Tortugas, helped treat yellow-fever outbreak among inmates; was pardoned and released by President Andrew Johnson in 1869

Marshall W. Nirenberg (1927-   ), biochemist; awarded 1968 Nobel Prize in physiology or medicine for his work in proteins and genetics

Osceola (1803?-1838), Seminole leader; violently opposing removal of the Seminole from their land, he led their resistance early in the Second Seminole War (1835-42); in 1837 was betrayed and captured by General Thomas Jessup; died a prisoner at Fort Moultrie

Ruth Bryan Owen (1855-1954), politician, diplomat; represented Florida in the United States House of Representatives (1929-33), becoming the first congresswoman from the Deep South; as United States minister to Denmark (1933-36) became the first American woman diplomat; served as alternate United States representative to the United Nations General Assembly (1949)

John D. Pennekamp (1898-1978), editor of *Miami Herald* and staunch conservationist whose efforts led to the creation of Everglades National Park and the nation's first underwater park, a 75,000-acre (30,352-hectare) preserve off Key Largo that is named in his honor

Henry Perrine (1797-1840), physician and botanist; introduced several useful tropical plants to south Florida, including henequen and sisal; killed by Indians who were seeking his neighbor, Jacob Housman, in the Florida Keys

Henry B. Plant (1819-1899), railroad and hotel magnate; developer of Florida's west coast and founder of shipping line bearing his name.

Juan Ponce de León (1460-1521), Spanish explorer; landed on Florida's east coast in April of 1513, named the area *Florida*, and claimed it for Spain; returned to colonize the region in 1521, but was wounded fatally during an Indian attack

Philip A. Randolph (1889-1979), born in Crescent City; labor and civil-rights leader; founded Brotherhood of Sleeping Car Porters Union

Marjorie Kinnan Rawlings (1896-1953), author; received 1939 Pulitzer Prize in fiction for her novel *The Yearling*; settled in Cross Creek near Ocala National Forest and became eloquent advocate for rural life in central Florida

Mary Martha Reid (1812-1894), nurse; promoted better care for Florida's wounded soldiers throughout Civil War; first chapter of the United Daughters of the Confederacy named for her

Burt Reynolds (1936-   ), actor; grew up in Jupiter; best-known films include *Deliverance* and *Smokey and the Bandit*; developer of Burt Reynolds Dinner Theatre in Jupiter

Jean Ribault (1520-1565), French Huguenot naval officer, explorer, and colonizer; in 1565 he was sent to reinforce the new French colony at Fort Caroline; while he was on his way to attack the Spanish at St. Augustine, Menéndez and his forces marched overland and captured Fort Caroline; when Ribault's fleet was wrecked in a storm, he was captured and executed by Menéndez

JOHN D. PENNEKAMP

JUAN PONCE DE LEÓN

PHILIP A. RANDOLPH

MARJORIE RAWLINGS

JOHN RINGLING

CHARLES SUMMERALL

John Ringling (1866-1936), circus entrepreneur; created Ringling Museum of Art in Sarasota and a spectacular residence he called *C'ad'zan*

Joseph Warren Stilwell (1883-1946), born in Palatka; military leader; commanded United States forces in China-Burma-India theater during World War II; nicknamed "Vinegar Joe" for his outspokenness

Harriet Beecher Stowe (1811-1896), author; lived in Mandarin; wrote articles about Florida for northern newspapers; best known as author of the anti-slavery novel *Uncle Tom's Cabin*

Charles Pelot Summerall (1867-1955), born in Lake City; military leader, educator; commanded forces in France during World War I; United States Army chief of staff (1926-30); president of Citadel, The Military College of South Carolina (1931-53)

Zachary Taylor (1784-1850), twelfth president of the United States; military leader; commanded American forces during the Second Seminole War (1837-40); president (1850-53)

Vincente Martinez Ybor (1818-1896), industrialist; a Cuban, Ybor established the cigar-making industry in Key West (1880) and later Tampa

David Levy Yulee (1811-1886), one of the first two United States senators from Florida (1845-51); directed construction of the first cross-state railroad

GOVERNORS

William D. Moseley	1845-1849	Sidney J. Catts	1917-1921
Thomas Brown	1849-1853	Cary A. Hardee	1921-1925
James E. Broome	1853-1857	John W. Martin	1925-1929
Madison S. Perry	1857-1861	Doyle E. Carlton	1929-1933
John Milton	1861-1865	David Sholtz	1933-1937
Abraham K. Allison	1865	Fred P. Cone	1937-1941
William Marvin	1865-1866	Spessard L. Holland	1941-1945
David S. Walker	1866-1868	Millard F. Caldwell	1945-1949
Harrison Reed	1868-1873	Fuller Warren	1949-1953
Ossian B. Hart	1873-1874	Dan T. McCarty	1953
Marcellus L. Stearns	1874-1877	Charley E. Johns	1953-1955
George F. Drew	1877-1881	LeRoy Collins	1955-1961
William D. Bloxham	1881-1885	Farris Bryant	1961-1965
Edward A. Perry	1885-1889	Haydon Burns	1965-1967
Francis P. Fleming	1889-1893	Claude Kirk, Jr.	1967-1971
Henry L. Mitchell	1893-1897	Reubin Askew	1971-1979
William D. Bloxham	1897-1901	Robert Graham	1979-1987
William S. Jennings	1901-1905	Robert Martinez	1987-
Napoleon B. Broward	1905-1909		
Albert W. Gilchrist	1909-1913		
Park Trammell	1913-1917		

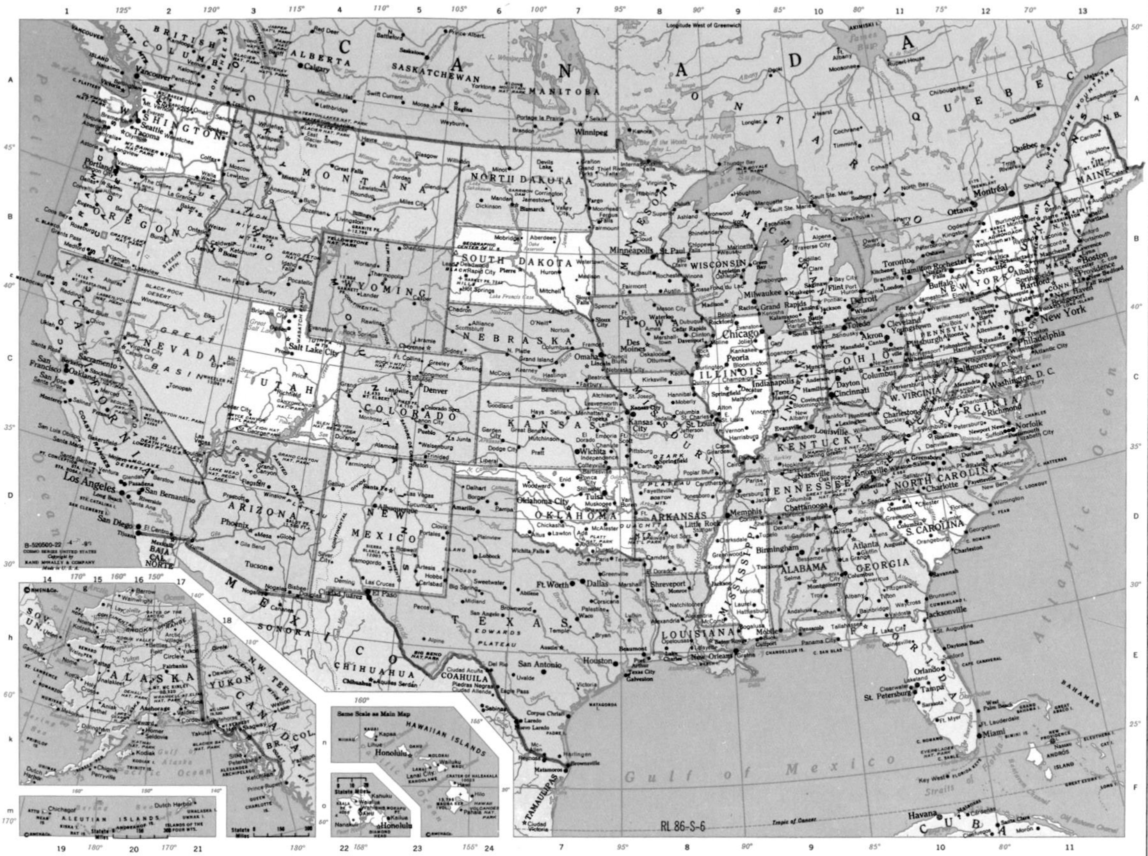
CANADA
BRITISH COLUMBIA
ALBERTA
SASKATCHEWAN
MANITOBA
ONTARIO
QUEBEC
WASHINGTON
OREGON
CALIFORNIA
NEVADA
IDAHO
MONTANA
WYOMING
UTAH
COLORADO
ARIZONA
NEW MEXICO
NORTH DAKOTA
SOUTH DAKOTA
NEBRASKA
KANSAS
OKLAHOMA
TEXAS
MINNESOTA
IOWA
MISSOURI
ARKANSAS
LOUISIANA
WISCONSIN
ILLINOIS
MICHIGAN
INDIANA
OHIO
KENTUCKY
TENNESSEE
MISSISSIPPI
ALABAMA
GEORGIA
FLORIDA
S. CAROLINA
NORTH CAROLINA
VIRGINIA
W. VIRGINIA
PENNSYLVANIA
NEW YORK
MAINE
MEXICO
SONORA
CHIHUAHUA
COAHUILA
ALASKA
YUKON
HAWAIIAN ISLANDS
ALEUTIAN ISLANDS
Gulf of Mexico
Atlantic Ocean
Pacific Ocean
CUBA
Havana
Seattle
Portland
San Francisco
Los Angeles
San Diego
Salt Lake City
Denver
Phoenix
Tucson
Minneapolis
Chicago
Detroit
Toronto
Montreal
Boston
New York
Philadelphia
Washington, D.C.
Atlanta
Miami
New Orleans
Houston
San Antonio
Dallas
Ft. Worth
Memphis
St. Louis
Kansas City
Oklahoma City
Winnipeg
Vancouver
Calgary
Honolulu
Same Scale as Main Map
RL 86-S-6

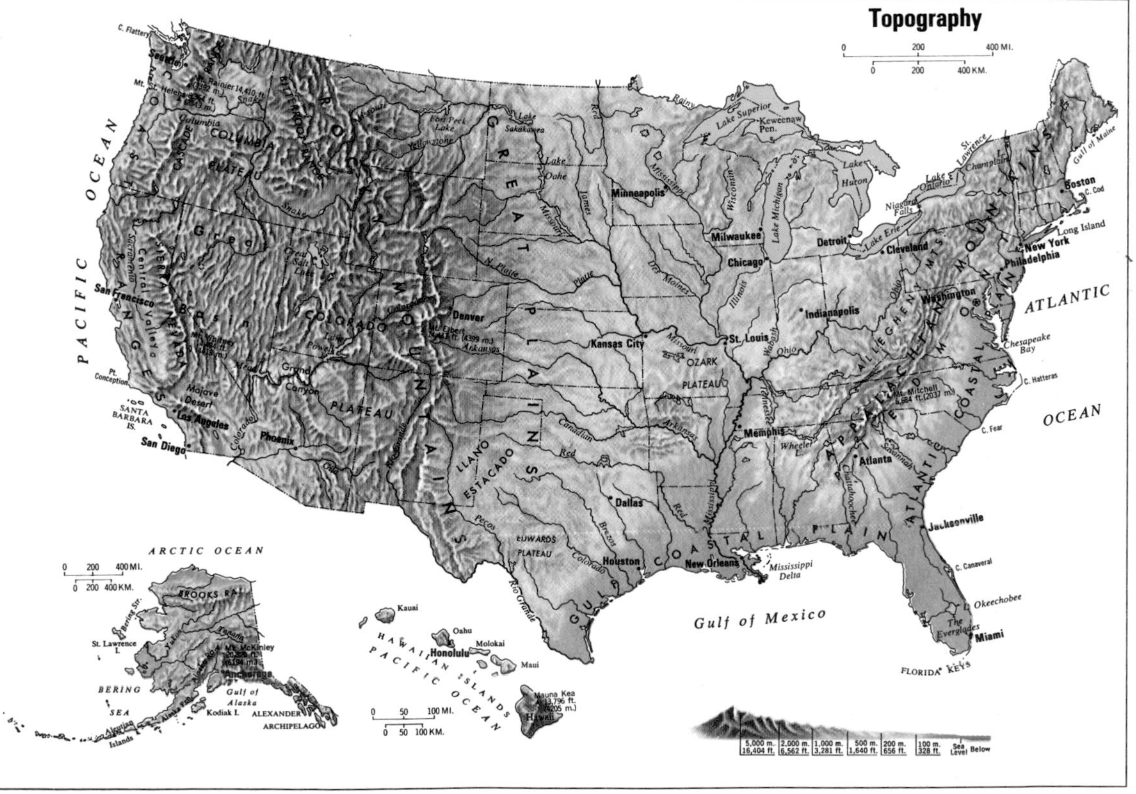
Topography
0 200 400 MI.
0 200 400 KM.
PACIFIC OCEAN
ATLANTIC OCEAN
Gulf of Mexico
ARCTIC OCEAN
BERING SEA
ROCKY MOUNTAINS
GREAT PLAINS
COLUMBIA PLATEAU
COLORADO PLATEAU
Great Basin
SIERRA NEVADA
COAST RANGES
CASCADE
LLANO ESTACADO
EDWARDS PLATEAU
OZARK PLATEAU
GULF COASTAL PLAIN
ATLANTIC COASTAL PLAIN
APPALACHIAN MTS.
Lake Superior
Lake Michigan
Lake Huron
Lake Erie
Lake Ontario
Mississippi
Missouri
Ohio
Rio Grande
Colorado
Mississippi Delta
Chesapeake Bay
C. Hatteras
C. Fear
C. Canaveral
C. Cod
Long Island
Niagara Falls
Okeechobee
The Everglades
FLORIDA KEYS
Seattle
San Francisco
Los Angeles
San Diego
Phoenix
Denver
Minneapolis
Milwaukee
Chicago
Detroit
Cleveland
Boston
New York
Philadelphia
Washington
Indianapolis
St. Louis
Kansas City
Memphis
Atlanta
Dallas
Houston
New Orleans
Jacksonville
Miami
Mt. Rainier 14,410 ft. (4392 m.)
Mt. Mitchell 6,684 ft. (2037 m.)
Mt. McKinley 20,320 ft. (6194 m.)
Mauna Kea 13,796 ft. (4205 m.)
BROOKS RA.
Yukon
Anchorage
Kodiak I.
ALEXANDER ARCHIPELAGO
St. Lawrence I.
Aleutian Islands
Gulf of Alaska
HAWAIIAN ISLANDS
Kauai
Oahu
Molokai
Maui
Hawaii
Honolulu
0 50 100 MI.
0 50 100 KM.
5,000 m. 16,404 ft.
2,000 m. 6,562 ft.
1,000 m. 3,281 ft.
500 m. 1,640 ft.
200 m. 656 ft.
100 m. 328 ft.
Sea Level
Below

MAP KEY

Alachua	C4
Altamonte Springs	D5
Anclote Keys (keys)	D4
Anna Maria Island (island)	q10
Apalachee Bay (bay)	B,C2,3
Apalachicola	C1
Apalachicola River (river)	B,C1,2
Apalachicola Bay (bay)	C1,2
Apopka	D5
Arcadia	E5
Atlantic Beach	m9
Atlantic Ocean	k,m,n9
Auburndale	D5
Aucilla River (river)	B3
Avon Park	E5
Banana River (river)	D6
Barnes Sound (sound)	G6
Bartow	E5
Bayshore Gardens	q10
Bee Ridge	q11
Belle Glade	F6
Belle Isle	D5
Belleair	p10
Big Cypress Swamp (swamp)	F5
Big Grass Island (island)	C3
Biscayne Bay (bay)	G6;s,t13
Biscayne Park	s13
Blackwater River (river)	u15
Blue Cypress Lake	E6
Boca Chica Key (key)	H5
Boca Ciega Bay (bay)	p10
Boca Raton	F6
Bonita Springs	F5
Bowling Green	E5
Boynton Beach	F6
Bradenton	E4;q10
Brandon	E4
Brent	u14
Brooksville	D4
Brownsville	S13
Cabbage Swamp (swamp)	m9
Caloosahatchee River (river)	F5
Canaveral National Seashore	D6
Cape Canaveral	D6
Cape Canaveral (cape)	D6
Cape Coral	F5
Cape Romano (cape)	G5
Cape San Blas (cape)	v16
Captiva Island (island)	F4
Carol City	s13
Casey Key (key)	E4
Casselberry	D5
Cedar Key (key)	C3
Chassahowitzka Bay (bay)	D4
Chattahoochee	B2
Chipley	u16
Chipola River (river)	B1
Choctawhatchee River (river)	u15,16
Choctawhatchee Bay (bay)	u15
Clearwater	E4;p10
Clermont	D5
Clewiston	F6
Cocoa	D6
Cocoa Beach	D6
Content Keys (keys)	H5
Conway	D5
Coral Gables	G6;s13
Corinne Key (key)	G5,6
Cortez	q10
Crestview	u15
Crook Lake (lake)	E5
Crystal Bay (bay)	D4
Crystal Lake	u16
Crystal Springs	D4
Cutler Ridge	s13
Cypress Lake (lake)	D5
Dade City	D4
Dania	F6;r13
Davie	F6;r13
Daytona Beach	C5
De Bary	D5
De Funiak Springs	u15
De Land	C5
Deerfield Beach	F6
Delray Beach	F6
Deltona	D5
Destin	u15
Dinner Point (point)	D4
Doctors Lake (lake)	m8
Dog Island (island)	C2
Dry Tortugas (islands)	H4
Dunedin	D4;o10
Durbin Creek (creek)	m8
Eagle Key (key)	G6
East Bay (bay)	u16
East Lake (lake)	D5
East Naples	F5
East Pass (pass)	C2
Econfina River (river)	B3
Edgewater	D6
Edmont Channel (channel)	p10
Edmont Key (key)	p10
Elliot Key (key)	G6;t13
Englewood	F4
Ensley	u14
Escambria River (river)	u14
Estero Bay (bay)	F5
Estero Island (island)	F5
Eustis	D5
Everglades, The (swamp)	F,G5,6
Everglades National Park	G5,6
False Cape (cape)	D6
Fernandina Beach	B5;k9
Fisheating Creek (creek)	F5
Florida Bay (bay)	H6
Florida City	G6;t13
Florida Keys (keys)	G,H5,6
Fort Lauderdale	F6;r13
Fort Meade	E5
Fort Myers	F5
Fort Myers Beach	F5
Fort Pierce	E6
Fort Pierce Inlet (inlet)	E6
Fort Walton Beach	u15
Frostproof	E5
Fruitville	E4;q11
Gainesville	C4
Gifford	E6
Gonzalez	u14
Goulds	s13
Green Cove Springs	C5;n8
Greenacres City	F6
Gulf Islands National Seashore	u14
Gulf of Mexico	p10;u,v14,15,16
Gulfport	E4;p10
Gullivan Bay (bay)	G5
Haines City	D5
Hallandale	G6;s13
Harlem	F6
Havana	B2
Hialeah	G6;s13
Highland Point (point)	G5
Hillsboro Canal (canal)	F6
Hillsborough (bay)	p10,11
Hobe Sound (sound)	E6
Hog Island (island)	C3
Holly Hill	C5
Hollywood	F6;r13
Homestead	G6;t13
Homosassa	D4
Horseshoe Point (point)	C3
Hudson	D4
Hutchinson Island (island)	E6
Immokalee	F5
Indian River (river)	D6
Indian Bay (bay)	D4
Indian Prairie Canal (canal)	E5
Indian Rocks Beach	p10
Indiantown	E6
Inverness	D4
Jacksonville	B5;m8
Jacksonville Beach	B5;m9
Jasmine Estates	D4
Jena	C3
Jenson Beach	E6
Johns Pass (pass)	p10
Jupiter	F6
Jupiter Inlet (inlet)	F6
Kendall	s13
Key Biscayne	s13
Key Largo	G6
Key West	H5
Kissimmee	D5
Kissimmee River (river)	E5
Lake Alfred	D5
Lake Apopka (lake)	D5
Lake Arbuckle (lake)	E5
Lake City	B4
Lake Dexter (lake)	C5
Lake George (lake)	C5
Lake Harney (lake)	D5
Lake Harris (lake)	D5
Lake Hart (lake)	D5
Lake Hatchineha (lake)	D5
Lake Iamonia (lake)	B2
Lake Ingraham (lake)	G5
Lake Istokpoga (lake)	E5
Lake Jackson (lake)	E5
Lake Jessup (lake)	D5
Lake June in Winter (lake)	E5
Lake Kerr (lake)	C5
Lake Kissimmee (lake)	E5
Lake Louisa (lake)	D5
Lake Magdalene	o11
Lake Marian (lake)	E5
Lake Miccosukee (lake)	B2
Lake Okeechobee (lake)	E,F5,6
Lake Park	F6
Lake Pierce (lake)	E5
Lake Placid (lake)	E5
Lake Poinsett (lake)	D6
Lake Tarpon (lake)	o10
Lake Tohopekaliga (lake)	D5
Lake Trafford (lake)	F5
Lake Wales	E5
Lake Washington (lake)	D5
Lake Weir (lake)	C5
Lake Weohyakapka (lake)	E5
Lake Worth	F6
Lake Worth Inlet (inlet)	F6
Lakeland	D5
Lantana	F6
Largo	E4;p10
Lauderdale Lakes	r13
Laurel	E4
Lealman	p10
Leesburg	D5
Lehigh Acres	F5
Leisure City	t13
Levy Lake (lake)	C4
Lighthouse Point (point)	C2
Little Manatee River (river)	p11
Live Oak	B3,4
Long Key (key)	H6
Long Pond (lake)	C4
Longboat Key (key)	E4;q10
Longboat Pass (pass)	q10
Lower Matecumbe Key (key)	H6
Lutz	D4
Lynn Haven	u16
Macclenny	B4
Manatee River (river)	E4;p11
Marco	G5
Margate	F6
Marianna	B1
Marathon	H5
Marquesas Keys (keys)	H4
Matanzas Inlet (inlet)	C5
Melbourne	D6
Memphis	p10
Merritt Island	D6
Miami	G6;s13
Miami Beach	G6;s13
Miami Canal (canal)	F,G6;r,s12,13
Miami Shores	G6;s13
Miami Springs	G6;s13
Milton	u14
Mims	D6
Miramar	s13
Mosquito Lagoon (lagoon)	D6
Mount Dora	D5
Mullet Key (key)	p10
Myakka River (river)	E4
Myrtle Grove	u14
Naples	F5
Naranja	G6;s13
Nassau River (river)	k8
Neptune Beach	B5;m9
New Port Richey	D4
New Smyrna Beach	C6
Newmans Lake (lake)	C4
Niceville	u15
Nokomis	E4
Norland	s13
North Fort Myers	F5
North Miami	G6;s13
North Miami Beach	s13
North Naples	F5
North New River Canal (canal)	F6;r13
Oakland Park	F6;r13
Ocala	C4
Ocean City	u15
Ochlockonee River (river)	B,C2
Ocoee	D5
Okeechobee	E6
Oklawaha River (river)	C5
Old Rhodes Key (key)	G6
Old Tampa Bay (bay)	p10
Olustee	B4
Oneco	E4;q10
Opa-Locka	s13
Orange Lake (lake)	C4
Orange Park	B5;m8
Orlando	D5
Ormond Beach	C5
Oyster Keys (keys)	G5,6
Pace	u14
Pahokee	F6
Palatka	C5
Palm Bay	D6
Palm Beach	F6
Palm Harbor	o10
Palmetto	E4;p10
Panama City	u16
Parker	u16
Pavilion Key (key)	G5
Peace River (river)	E5
Pembroke Pines	r13
Pensacola	u14
Pensacola Bay (bay)	u14,15
Perdido River (river)	u14
Perdido Bay (bay)	u14
Perrine	G6;s13
Perry	B3
Pine Castle	D5
Pine Hills	D5
Pine Island (island)	F4
Pine Island Sound (sound)	F4
Pine Key (key)	p10
Pinellas Park	E4;p10
Plant City	D4
Plantation	r13
Pompano Beach	F6;r13
Ponce de Leon Bay (bay)	G5
Ponce de Leon Inlet (inlet)	C6
Port Charlotte	F4
Port Orange	C6
Port Salerno	E6
Port St. Joe	C1;v16
Port St. Lucie	E6
Punta Gorda	F4
Quincy	B2
Reedy Lake (lake)	E5
Richmond Heights	s13
Riviera Beach	F6
Rock Island (island)	C3
Rockledge	D6
Ruskin	E4;p11
Safety Harbor	E4;p10
St. Andrew Bay (bay)	u16
St. Augustine	C5;n9
St. Cloud	D5
St. George Island (island)	C2
St. Johns River (river)	B,C,D5;m8
St. Joseph Bay (bay)	C1;u16
St. Joseph Sound (sound)	o10
St. Lucie Canal (canal)	E,F6
St. Lucie Inlet (inlet)	E6
St. Marys River (river)	B5
St. Petersburg	E4;p10
St. Petersburg Beach	p10
St. Vincent Island (island)	C1
Samoset	q11
Sand Key (key)	E4;p10
Sands Key (key)	s,t13
Sanford	D5
Sanibel	F4
Sanibel Island (island)	F4
Sarasota	E4;q10
Sarasota Bay (bay)	E4;q10
Sebastian Inlet (inlet)	E6
Sebring	E5
Sharpes	D6
Siesta Key (key)	E4;q10
Snipe Keys (keys)	H5
Soldier Key (key)	s13
South Bay	F6
South Daytona	C5
South Miami	G6;s13
South Miami Heights	s13
South New River Canal (canal)	r12,13
South Patrick Shores	D6
South Venice	E4
Southwest Channel (channel)	E4;p10
Spring Hill	D4
Springfield	u16
Starke	C4
Steinhatchee River (river)	C3
Straits of Florida	G,H6,7
Stuart	E6
Summerland Key (key)	H5
Sun City	p11
Surfside	s13
Suwannee River (river)	B,C3,4
Suwannee Sound (sound)	C3
Sweetwater Creek	p10
Talbot Island (island)	B5;m9
Tallahassee	B2
Tamiami Canal (canal)	F,G5,6;s12,13
Tampa	E4;p11
Tampa Bay (bay)	E4;p,q10
Tarpon Springs	D4
Tavares	D5
Tavernier	G6
Temple Terrace	o11
Ten Thousand Islands (islands)	F5
Thomas Creek (creek)	k,m8
Tice	F5
Titusville	D6
Trout River (river)	m8
Tsala Apopka Lake (lake)	D4
Vaca Key (key)	H5
Valparaiso	u15
Venice	E4
Vero Beach	E6
Waccasassa (bay)	C4
Warrington	u14
Watertown	B4
West Bay (bay)	u16
West Miami	s13
West Palm Beach	F6
West Pensacola	u14
Westwood Lakes	s13
White City	E6
Whitefield Estates	q10
Whitewater Bay (bay)	G5,6
Winston	D4
Winter Garden	D5
Winter Haven	D5
Winter Park	D5
Withlacoochee River (river)	B3
Yellow River (river)	u15
Yulee	B5;k8
Zephyrhills	D4

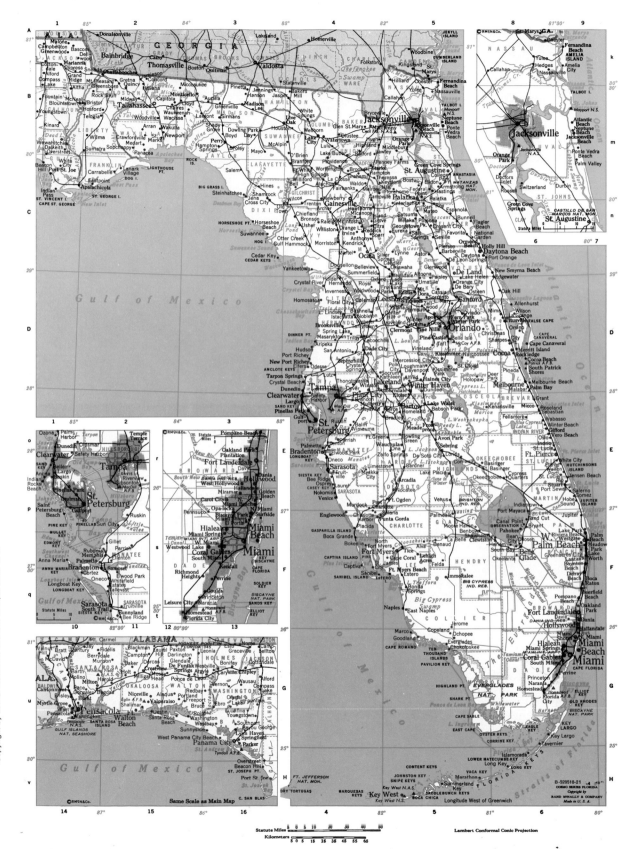

Statute Miles

Kilometers

Lambert Conformal Conic Projection

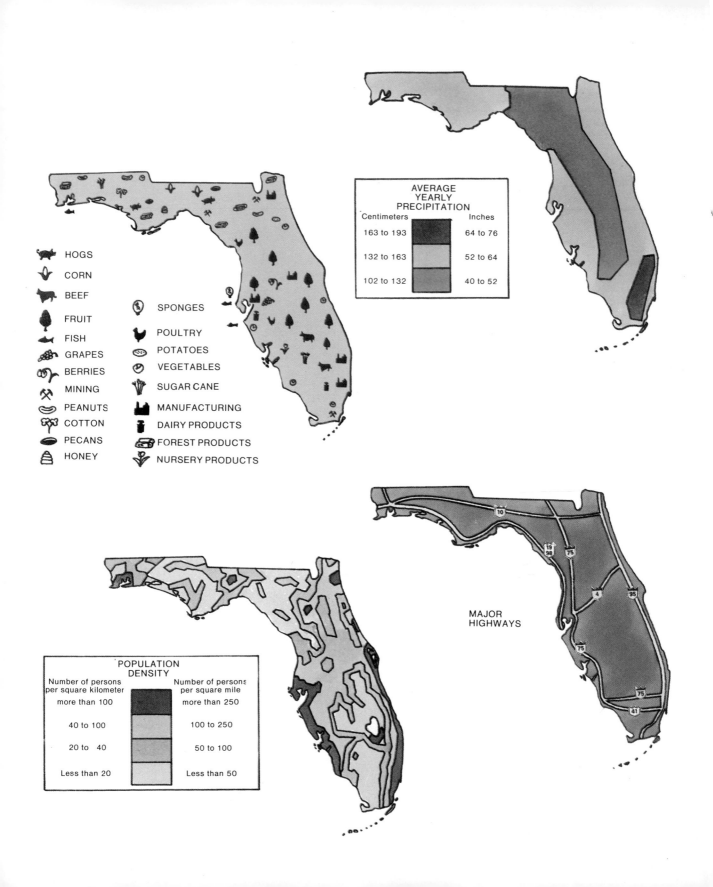

HOGS

CORN

BEEF

FRUIT

FISH

GRAPES

BERRIES

MINING

PEANUTS

COTTON

PECANS

HONEY

SPONGES

POULTRY

POTATOES

VEGETABLES

SUGAR CANE

MANUFACTURING

DAIRY PRODUCTS

FOREST PRODUCTS

NURSERY PRODUCTS

AVERAGE
YEARLY
PRECIPITATION

Centimeters		Inches
163 to 193		64 to 76
132 to 163		52 to 64
102 to 132		40 to 52

POPULATION
DENSITY

Number of persons per square kilometer		Number of persons per square mile
more than 100		more than 250
40 to 100		100 to 250
20 to 40		50 to 100
Less than 20		Less than 50

MAJOR
HIGHWAYS

TOPOGRAPHY

Perdido R.
Escambia R.
Pensacola
Pensacola Bay
Santa Rosa I.
345 ft.
(105 m.)
L. Seminole
Choctawhatchee
Apalachicola
Ochlockonee
Tallahassee
Apalachee Bay
C. San Blas
C. St. George
Okefenokee Swamp
St. Marys
Suwannee
Jacksonville
St. Johns
Daytona Beach
L. George
Tsala Apopka L.
Withlacoochee R.
L. Apopka
Orlando
Merritt I.
C. Canaveral
Iron Mtn. 325 ft. (99 m.)
L. Kissimmee
Tampa
St. Petersburg
Tampa Bay
Peace R.
Kissimmee R.
Lake Okeechobee
West Palm Beach
Charlotte Har.
Caloosahatchee
Fort Myers
Big Cypress Swamp
Fort Lauderdale
Tamiami Canal
The Everglades
TEN THOUSAND IS.
Miami
Biscayne Bay
C. Sable
Whitewater Bay
Key Largo
Florida Bay
Dry Tortugas
Marquesas Keys
Key West
FLORIDA KEYS

| 5,000 m. 16,404 ft. | 2,000 m. 6,562 ft. | 1,000 m. 3,281 ft. | 500 m. 1,640 ft. | 200 m. 656 ft. | 100 m. 328 ft. | Sea Level | Below |

Courtesy of Hammond, Incorporated
Maplewood, New Jersey

COUNTIES

ESCAMBIA
SANTA ROSA
Milton
OKALOOSA
Crestview
De Funiak Springs
HOLMES
Bonifay
WALTON
Chipley
WASHINGTON
Marianna
JACKSON
Blountstown
Quincy
GADSDEN
Bristol
LIBERTY
CALHOUN
Panama City
BAY
GULF
Port St. Joe
Apalachicola
FRANKLIN
WAKULLA
Crawfordville
TALLAHASSEE
LEON
Monticello
JEFFERSON
Madison
MADISON
Perry
TAYLOR
Mayo
LAFAYETTE
Live Oak
SUWANNEE
HAMILTON
Jasper
COLUMBIA
Lake City
UNION
Lake Butler
BAKER
Macclenny
NASSAU
Fernandina Beach
DUVAL
Jacksonville
Starke
BRADFORD
CLAY
Green Cove Springs
ST. JOHNS
St. Augustine
Cross City
DIXIE
Trenton
GILCHRIST
Bronson
ALACHUA
Gainesville
Palatka
PUTNAM
Bunnell
FLAGLER
LEVY
MARION
Ocala
De Land
VOLUSIA
CITRUS
Inverness
SUMTER
Bushnell
LAKE
Tavares
Sanford
SEMINOLE
ORANGE
Orlando
Titusville
Brooksville
HERNANDO
Dade City
PASCO
Kissimmee
OSCEOLA
BREVARD
Clearwater
PINELLAS
Tampa
HILLSBOROUGH
POLK
Bartow
INDIAN RIVER
Vero Beach
Bradenton
MANATEE
Sarasota
SARASOTA
Arcadia
DE SOTO
HARDEE
Wauchula
Sebring
HIGHLANDS
OKEECHOBEE
Okeechobee
Ft. Pierce
ST. LUCIE
Stuart
MARTIN
Punta Gorda
CHARLOTTE
Ft. Myers
LEE
GLADES
Moore Haven
HENDRY
La Belle
West Palm Beach
PALM BEACH
Naples
COLLIER
BROWARD
Ft. Lauderdale
Miami
DADE
MONROE
Key West

Vacationers relaxing on a beach in the Florida Keys

INDEX

Page numbers that appear in boldface type indicate illustrations

These Seminole women, shown here in traditional dress, are among the approximately fifteen hundred Seminole who still live in Florida.

Picture Identifications
Front cover: Miami Beach
Back cover: Fakahatchee Strand
Pages 2-3: Sand dunes along the Gulf Coast in northwest Florida
Page 6: Tourists swimming in the Gulf of Mexico off the west coast of Florida
Page 8-9: Cypress trees along Santa Fe Lake
Page 26: Montage of the various types of people who live and work in Florida
Pages 34-35: Florida Indians as portrayed by sixteenth-century French artist Jacques le Moyne
Page 48: Seminole leader Osceola
Page 60: 1915 photo showing the first automobile to reach Miami
Page 72: The old and new state capitol buildings in Tallahassee
Pages 82-83: Rafting in Jacksonville
Pages 94-95: Everglades National Park
Page 95 (inset): Fishing pier in Naples at sunset
Page 108: Montage showing the state flower (orange blossom), the state flag, the state shell (Florida horse conch), the state mammal in salt water (dolphin), the state bird (mockingbird), and the state tree (sabal palm)

About the Author

Lynn M. Stone was born and raised in Connecticut. He received his undergraduate degree from Aurora College in Illinois and his master's degree from Northern Illinois University. A teacher, writer, and outdoor photographer, he has authored eleven books for young people, as well as numerous articles. His photographs have appeared in dozens of books and seventy different magazines. As a former resident of Sarasota who has traveled extensively throughout Florida, Mr. Stone says he feels like a semi-native: "I've had mangrove mud between my toes, sand in my shoes, and a wicked sunburn or two. I feel like I belong."

Picture Acknowledgments

H. Armstrong Roberts, Inc.: Pages 4, 69 (left); Camerique: Front cover; © W. Metzen: Pages 8-9, 15, 20 (left), 42, 72, 75 (left), 82-83, 97, 105; © T. Altstiel: Page 14 (right); © H. G. Ross: Page 89; © W. Bertsch: Pages 94-95, 138
© **Mary Ann Brockman:** Pages 2-3
© **Chip and Rosa Maria Peterson:** Pages 5, 14 (left)
© **Lynn M. Stone:** Pages 6, 11, 17 (left), 18, 19 (right), 21 (both photos), 22 (snake, panther), 25 (right), 78, 86 (right), 91 (bottom left), 102, 106 (right), 108 (sabal palm, orange blossom, horse conch), 115
Tom Stack & Associates: © Matt Bradley: Pages 13 (left), 22 (crab), 81, 103; © Joe & Carol McDonald: Page 22 (roseate spoonbill); © Brian Parker: Page 22 (alligator, turtles); © Jeff Foott: Page 22 (manatees); © John Cancalosi: Page 22 (deer); © F. Stuart Westmorland: Page 25 (left); © M. Timothy O'Keefe: Pages 85 (left), 141; © Herb Segars: Page 85 (right); © Tom Stack: Page 108 (dolphin)
R/C Agency: © Earl L. Kubis: Page 13 (top right); © J. Madeley: Page 95 (inset)
Nawrocki Stock Photo: © Les Van: Pages 13 (bottom right), 26 (center); © Jeffrey Apoian: Pages 26 (bottom left), 91 (top left); © C. Sissac: Page 86 (left); © Wm. S. Nawrocki: Page 106 (left)
© **Pat Canova:** Pages 17 (right), 113
Root Resources: © Bill Glass: Page 19 (left); © Jim Nachel: Page 22 (purple gallinule); © MacDonald Photography: Pages 26 (bottom right), 31 (left); © Gordon and Janet Groene: Page 64 (right); © Bill Barksdale: Page 77 (right); © Lia Munson: Page 99
© **Cameramann International Ltd.:** Pages 20 (right), 26 (top left), 76, 77 (left), 91 (bottom right), 117, 118
© **Virginia Grimes:** Page 26 (middle left)
© **Joan Dunlop:** Page 26 (top right), 69 (right)
© **Joseph A. DiChello, Jr.:** Pages 26 (bottom center), 31 (right), 64 (left), 75 (right)
© **Southern Stock Photos:** © Wendell Metzen: Page 28
Wide World Photos: Pages 32, 60, 63, 70, 127 (Benjamin), 128 (all photos), 129 (M. Fisher, Hemingway, Hurston), 130 (Kirk, Nirenberg), 131 (Pennekamp, Randolph, Rawlings), 132 (both photos)
Historical Pictures Service Inc., Chicago: Pages 34-35, 37, 39 (both photos), 40 (all photos), 45, 46, 48, 50, 57, 58, 66 (both photos), 127 (Bethune), 129 (Jackson), 130 (Lanier, Menéndez), 131 (Ponce de León)
The Bettmann Archive: Page 55
Photri: Page 67
Marilyn Gartman Agency: © Michael Philip Manheim: Pages 91 (top right), 100
Courtesy Flag Research Center, Winchester, Massachusetts 01890: Flag on page 108
© **James P. Rowan:** Pages 108 (mockingbird), 112
© **Jerry Hennen:** Page 123
Len W. Meents: Maps on pages 97, 99, 100, 103, 105, 136
The Image Bank: © J. H. Carmichael: Back cover